THE BUSY PROFESSIONAL'S GUIDE TO

PASSIVE APARTMENT INVESTING

A TIME-EFFICIENT FRAMEWORK TO EVALUATE DEALS, REDUCE RISK, AND INVEST SMARTER IN REAL ESTATE

VESSI KAPOULIAN

Copyright © 2026 by Vessela (Vessi) Kapoulian. All Rights Reserved.

The Busy Professional's Guide to Passive Apartment Investing
(A Time-Efficient Framework to Evaluate Deals, Reduce Risk, and Invest Smarter in Real Estate)

All rights reserved. No part of this publication may be reproduced, distributed or transmitted in any form or by any means, including photocopying, recording, or other electronic or mechanical methods, without the prior written permission of the publisher, except in the case of brief quotations embodied in critical reviews and certain other noncommercial uses permitted by copyright law.

Although the author and publisher have made every effort to ensure that the information in this book was correct at press time, the author and publisher do not assume and hereby disclaim any liability to any party for any loss, damage, or disruption caused by errors or omissions, whether such errors or omissions result from negligence, accident, or any other cause.

Adherence to all applicable laws and regulations, including international, federal, state and local governing professional licensing, business practices, advertising, and all other aspects of doing business in the US, Canada or any other jurisdiction is the sole responsibility of the reader and consumer.

Neither the author nor the publisher assumes any responsibility or liability whatsoever on behalf of the consumer or reader of this material. Any perceived slight of any individual or organization is purely unintentional.

The resources in this book are provided for informational purposes only and should not be used to replace the specialized training and professional judgment of a finance or legal professional.

ISBN: 979-8-90057-365-6 - Ebook
ISBN: 979-8-90057-366-3 - Paperback
ISBN: 979-8-90057-367-0 - Hardcover
ISBN: 979-8-90057-368-7 - Audiobook

Disclaimer

The content in the book represents the views, opinions, and experiences of the author and is not intended to serve as individual tax, legal, financial, or investment advice.

To my brother, Gary Kapulyan:

Some people move through life leaving everyone they touch better for having known them. You are that person. Your kindness to everyone, your instinct to care for others, and the love you pour into your family make you one of the most inspiring people I know. As a brother, son, husband, and father, you lead with heart, grace, and quiet strength. I do not know what I did to deserve you, but I thank God every day that I did.

CONTENTS

Appendix

INSIDER'S KIT

To access the complimentary resources that accompany this book, go to:

www.dbacapitalgroup.com/book-resources.

For additional guidance on multifamily investing, go here: www.dbacapitalgroup.com

HOW THIS BOOK WORKS

Each topic represents a brief read that covers the basic but key concepts to arm you with the knowledge needed to embark on your investment journey. The chapters are intended to stand on their own and therefore can be used as a reference.

Each chapter blends teaching with application. You will find mini case studies/stories, checklists, and access to additional resources throughout the book. Finally, for ease of reference a summary of key terminology is also provided in the Glossary (see the Appendix).

Lastly, a great companion to this book (especially for those looking to gain deeper understanding of how to vet apartment deals from A to Z with confidence and ease) is **Mastering Multifamily Underwriting (5 Steps to Confident Risk-Smart Apartment Investing)**. You can get your copy on Amazon or find out more about it here: www.MasteringMultifamilyUnderwriting.com/book.

YOUR JOURNEY AHEAD

By the time you finish this book, you will no longer look at a deal the same way. You will know how to assess the lead sponsor, test the numbers and each assumption, understand the market, pierce through key deal structure points, and decide with confidence whether a deal is worth your capital.

More than that, you will see yourself differently. You will not be a passive follower at the mercy of someone else's spreadsheet. You will be an informed, empowered investor with a process you can trust.

That is the transformation waiting for you inside these pages. Let us begin.

P.S. Any additional resources referenced throughout the chapters below, you can also locate at the book resource page here: www.dbacapitalgroup.com/book-resources.

PRELUDE TO THE SECOND EDITION

When the first edition of this book was published, the goal was simple: to help busy professionals understand how to evaluate passive multifamily investments without feeling overwhelmed. The framework presented in those pages was built on fundamentals - disciplined underwriting, thoughtful market selection, and a clear understanding of risk.

Those fundamentals have not changed.

However, the real estate environment has.

Over the past few years, the multifamily market has experienced one of the most dramatic shifts in decades. Interest rates rose rapidly, financing structures that once appeared benign revealed their hidden risks, and many deals that looked attractive on paper began to struggle under pressure.

In many cases, the underlying issue was not the asset itself. The problem was the assumptions.

Deals that relied on aggressive rent growth, short-term floating rate debt, thin reserves, or optimistic exit pricing have faced significant challenges. By contrast, investments built on conservative underwriting, adequate reserves, and prudent leverage have generally been far more resilient.

Some lead sponsors fought tooth and nail to protect their investors and save the deal. By contrast, others walked away or resorted to fraud.

In other words, the principles outlined in the first edition were not theoretical. They were stress tested in real time.

This second edition does not replace the original framework. Instead, it expands upon it. The core concepts remain the same, but this edition incorporates updated market data, lessons learned from the recent market cycle, and additional insights that can help investors better identify both opportunities and risks.

For readers who followed the discipline outlined in the first edition, the recent market turbulence likely reinforced the importance of those principles.

For those who did not, the past few years have provided a powerful reminder that real estate investing rewards patience, discipline, and risk awareness.

My hope is that this updated edition continues to serve as a practical guide - one that helps investors approach passive multifamily investing with clarity, confidence, and a healthy respect for risk.

Because while markets change, sound investment principles rarely do.

PART 1

ORIENTATION: THE BIG PICTURE

CHAPTER 1

INTRODUCTION

I grew up in Bulgaria, behind the Iron Curtain. At that time, there was no stock market and investing in hard assets was the only real investment one would consider. Typically, that meant being able to purchase your own home, possibly a second home, and gold/silver in the form of jewelry. It was not until I came to the US that I discovered the popularity of the stock market. Nevertheless, I never fully warmed up to it as in my own little mind at the time, it resembled a large casino, and I am not a fan of gambling.

I followed the traditional path of going to school, then grad school, getting a corporate job, and making it my mission to climb the corporate ladder. After a few years, however, I realized I was climbing the wrong ladder. When I looked up, I saw people trading their time for money. A promotion meant less time with family and loved ones. Other clues were present all along the way too – it just took me a little while to see them. (1) The 2008-09 market crash, which left some people, including those ready to retire, with collapsed retirement plan values and many others without a job. (2) My own employer went through a couple of restructures. I was spared. However, at that moment I knew that I could be next as, in my humble view, I was not any more special than the colleagues who were let go. If anything, it was probably an indicator that I was getting paid less.

Thankfully I picked up the lessons eventually and decided to take action. I could not control the global markets or corporate restructures. However, I could control how I prepare for retirement and start building my own financial freedom. In those moments of crisis, I resorted to what I knew growing up – investing in hard assets and real estate. The seed of real estate planted in me back then started to germinate. And so, I got to work.

One day I stumbled across a real estate seminar. I took the day off work to attend. It ultimately ended up being an upsell. However, I took good notes and walked out of the seminar building my own deal analysis templates and taking the next step into my real estate journey. A bit later, I came across a local real estate investment club where one of the speakers was consistently holding meet ups and educational presentations without the sales pitch. One day I picked up the phone and called him to inquire whether he also sells properties or knows of someone who sells properties. He did. And before you know it, I had purchased my first investment property out of state. It took a bit longer to stabilize but I quickly started seeing the benefit of good underwriting and selecting the right location in the form of steady monthly cash flow.

Within a couple of years, I purchased another property in the same market and subsequently diversified to another state. The properties had been performing and this prompted me to ask the question – how do I scale this further? This led me to look into multifamily. I devoured tons of educational content and invested in a coaching program/mastermind that most closely aligned with my goals. I kept moving forward and taking action.

It was not daisies and butterflies all along the way. There were challenges, obstacles, tough decisions, painful seminars, and valuable lessons learned. It has also been a lot of hustle and countless hours. However, it is through moments of adversity that one grows and becomes stronger.

One beautiful day I walked into my office. It was a normal day...or so it seemed. My day started with a meeting, which I thought would be a standard mid-year review. Instead, I was informed that our entire division is being closed and that as a result thereof, my team and I are being let go. My colleagues and I had less than 90 minutes to pack, say our goodbyes, and leave the building before computer and building access were shut down. Fifteen years of blood and sweat and dedication to the firm were wiped out just like that. A heartless kick in the behind and out the door.

It was always my intent to transition to real estate full time and start my own business at some point. The timeline was just accelerated with this event. The difference this time around, however, was that I was prepared. My real estate and passive income built over the past few years were my ally. I could survive. But I wanted to thrive. My burning desire to succeed and knowing this was possible based on prior experience led me to expand into other active and passive income streams.

I am now on a mission to help other high-achieving professionals and business owners protect the downside, build durable passive income, and create long-term optionality for their families.

I am energized by the opportunity to create lasting impact through education and to cultivate a community of disciplined, empowered investors.

Dream. Believe. Achieve. Always.

CHAPTER 2

CRAFTING YOUR ROADMAP

Before diving into the mechanics of investing, it is important to step back and establish a simple roadmap.

Many investors jump directly into evaluating deals, comparing returns, or chasing the latest opportunity that crosses their desk. In reality, the process should begin much earlier. The most effective investors start by clarifying ***why*** they are investing in the first place.

Real estate can serve different **purposes** depending on the individual. For some, the goal is to create reliable *passive income*. For others, it is *long-term wealth creation*, *tax efficiency*, *capital preservation*, or a *combination of all* of the above. Understanding what role real estate is meant to play in your life helps anchor every decision that follows.

Once the purpose is clear, the next step is to **define your investment goals**. These may include generating cash flow, pursuing appreciation, reducing tax liability, or protecting purchasing power by simply staying ahead of inflation. Most investors ultimately pursue a blend of these objectives, and the mix may evolve over time as their financial situation and priorities change.

With goals established, the next step is **selecting the investment vehicle**. Real estate offers many options - from single family homes to development, industrial, self-storage, and many others. This book focuses specifically on multifamily real estate (apartments), an asset class that has historically offered a balance of income, stability, and long-term growth.

Only after these foundational decisions are made should the tactical steps begin: educating yourself, building relationships with operators, evaluating opportunities, and gradually building a portfolio.

In the sections that follow, we will walk through this process in a practical way - starting with the mindset and framework that successful passive investors use, and then outlining the steps that can help you move forward with clarity and confidence.

Cash Flow vs. Appreciation vs. Tax Efficiencies – Why Not All?

You cannot get to where you need to get, if you do not know where you are headed. Or you may stumble along the way until you get on the path leading you to your desired destination. Having clear goals upfront is the first step of setting yourself up for success in achieving that goal. So are defining your investment strategy and criteria. Below I will share the three most common investment strategies.

Cash Flow

Later on in the book I will illustrate how an initial seed investment of $50K invested at very conservative returns can generate meaningful passive income streams over a period of time. If cash flow is your primary goal, it would be important to vet the deal (more on that later in CHAPTER 17 and 24) to ensure it produces the desired cash on cash return. One deal is definitely NOT going to replace your existing income stream. However, when compounded over a long period of time and when new investments are added to your portfolio, it can very well meet or exceed your current income. This requires patience (having at least a 10-year time horizon) and discipline (knowing how to analyze deals, adhering to your investment goals and criteria, and not chasing shiny objects).

Appreciation

If you are happy with your current cash flow from your W2 salary or other investments and if you are more risk tolerant, then you might be more attracted to investments with a great opportunity for appreciation. This is where wealth compounds. Examples of such would include new construction, distressed deals, flips, or land deals. Examples of such markets are Los Angeles, CA or New York, NY. Counting on appreciation is generally a riskier strategy and slightly more speculative as you are reliant on market dynamics outside of your control to deliver target returns. However, it might make sense if your risk tolerance is higher and you do not need the cash flow in the interim period until the asset is sold or refinanced. Appreciation is what creates the wealth building effect of real estate investing in the long run.

Tax savings

For high income earners, reduction in tax liability may be a higher priority vs. the prior two strategies. Such tax liability reduction (via deferral) would enable them to utilize the taxes saved for other purposes – business or personal. In that scenario, selecting an investment that reduces tax liability via depreciation or reduces capital gains via 1031 exchange might be the better solution (we cover that in more detail in Part 6).

All of the above

You do not have to limit yourself to only one strategy. In addition, your strategy can change over time based on your individual circumstances. Thus, you may decide to use a combination of all three.

Knowing your investment strategy and investment criteria will help you quickly prescreen various deals coming across your desk and pass on the ones outside of your investment box. Hopefully this will also make the investment process less overwhelming and reduce distractions, fear of missing out, or shiny objects that divert you from following your own path to financial freedom.

Five Steps to Start Investing in Real Estate Syndications with Confidence

I am often asked how one can begin investing passively in real estate and, over time, scale that approach into a meaningful source of passive income. For many new investors, the process can feel overwhelming at first. Real estate presents many opportunities, the terminology may be unfamiliar, and the minimum investment amounts are often significant.

The good news is that the path does not need to be complicated. By approaching passive investing with intention and focus, investors can build both the knowledge and the confidence necessary to make thoughtful decisions.

Below is a five-step roadmap that investors can follow at the beginning of their investment journey.

1. Choose Your Investment Vehicle

Real estate offers a wide range of investment opportunities. Investors may consider new development, single-family rentals, small or large multifamily properties, self-storage, industrial properties, hotels, retail centers, and many others.

For someone just starting out, this breadth of options can feel overwhelming.

After you take some time to understand what asset classes are available, choose one area to focus on initially and begin learning about it in greater depth. Staying focused early on helps reduce complexity and allows you to develop a clearer understanding of how that asset class performs across different market conditions.

This does not mean you should never diversify. In fact, diversification often becomes an important strategy later on. However, in the beginning, taking one step at a time can make the process far more manageable.

2. Educate Yourself and Learn the Landscape

Education is an ongoing process, particularly in markets influenced by changing economic, macroeconomic, and geopolitical conditions.

While sponsors typically provide a significant amount of information about each investment opportunity, as a steward of your own capital you have the responsibility to understand the risks involved, the mitigating factors, and how an investment aligns with your financial goals.

There are several effective ways to begin building this knowledge base:

- **Podcasts** – A great way for busy professionals to learn during commutes or spare moments throughout the day. There are many excellent real estate podcasts available that discuss market trends, underwriting, and investment strategies.
- **Books** – For those who enjoy reading, books provide a structured and comprehensive way to learn about real estate investing and financial principles.
- **Blogs and operator educational content** – Many operators publish educational articles and insights on their company websites. These can provide valuable perspectives on how deals are analyzed and executed.
- **Webinars and educational presentations** – These often allow investors to learn directly from experienced operators and industry professionals.
- **Investor groups, meetups, and conferences** – These events provide opportunities not only to learn, but also

to connect with other investors and hear about their real-world experiences.

Writing this book was inspired by my desire to help investors become more educated and empowered. I continue to share educational content at dbacapitalgroup.com and through my social media channels on LinkedIn, YouTube, Facebook, and Instagram. I also wrote a best-selling book that dives deeper into apartment deal analysis for investors new to multifamily (www.MasteringMultifamilyUnderwriting.com/Book).

Education builds confidence. Confidence leads to better decisions.

3. Understand Your Financial Position and Available Capital

Before making your first investment, it is important to have a clear understanding of your financial position and the capital you have available to invest.

Beyond excess liquidity or investable cash, investors may also have additional sources of capital, including:

- Self-directed retirement accounts
- Cash-out refinance proceeds
- Proceeds from a 1031 exchange

However, one important principle should always be kept in mind: **never risk your last dollar in your first investment.**

Unexpected life events happen. Markets change. Investments take time to mature. Maintaining a financial cushion allows you to respond to unforeseen circumstances without unnecessary stress.

Be honest and realistic about your financial situation. When taking risk, it should always be thoughtful and calculated.

4. Define Your Investment Criteria and Objectives

Before reviewing specific investment opportunities, it is helpful to clearly define what you are trying to accomplish.

Some investors prioritize **cash flow**, while others focus primarily on **long-term appreciation**. Many seek a combination of both.

You may also have additional objectives, such as:

- Building long-term wealth
- Generating passive income
- Reducing tax liability through depreciation and other tax advantages
- Preserving capital while achieving modest growth above inflation

It is also important to determine your **investment horizon**, whether that is short, medium, or long term, and to develop realistic expectations around potential returns.

Having a defined investment framework will make it significantly easier to evaluate opportunities and filter out deals that do not align with your goals.

5. Build Relationships with Operators, Take Action, and Track Results

One of the most important aspects of passive investing is developing relationships with the operators who sponsor and manage investments and building your deal pipeline. As discussed later in this book, the operator is often the single most important factor in determining whether an investment succeeds or fails.

There are several ways investors can begin getting to know operators and evaluating potential partners:

- **Schedule introductory calls or meetings** – Many sponsors provide access to their calendars so prospective investors can schedule a conversation. These discussions allow you to ask questions and begin building a relationship.
- **Subscribe to sponsor email lists and follow their content** – Over time, you will gain insight into their investment philosophy, communication style, and overall approach to the business.
- **Attend meetups, conferences, and investor events** – These are excellent venues for meeting operators and fellow investors in person.
- **Seek references from other investors** – Recommendations from trusted colleagues can be helpful, although they should never replace your own diligence.

At some point, however, it is important to move beyond research and begin taking action. Many investors fall into the trap of **analysis paralysis**, spending years studying investments without ever making their first one.

While it is wise to be patient and thoughtful, it is equally important to remember that building wealth takes time. Compounding works best when capital is invested over long periods.

Timing the market is extremely difficult, and attempting to perfectly predict market cycles often leads investors to remain on the sidelines indefinitely.

As the Chinese proverb wisely reminds us:

"The best time to plant a tree was twenty years ago. The next best time is today."

CHAPTER 3

WHY MULTIFAMILY?

I am often asked why I love multifamily as an asset class, given the multitude of other investment options or other real estate asset classes. There are a few reasons for this. While many of the factors below would apply to real estate in general, most references below are made to multifamily.

1. **Risk vs. return.** Multifamily has historically outperformed other asset classes, including during recessions. I will spare you the quant data analysis but have included a few interesting data charts below that support this conclusion and show that commercial real estate generates among the highest returns while maintaining a risk level near that of US government bonds.

Exhibit 1: Commercial Real Estate Has Delivered Strong Risk-Adjusted Returns in The Long Run

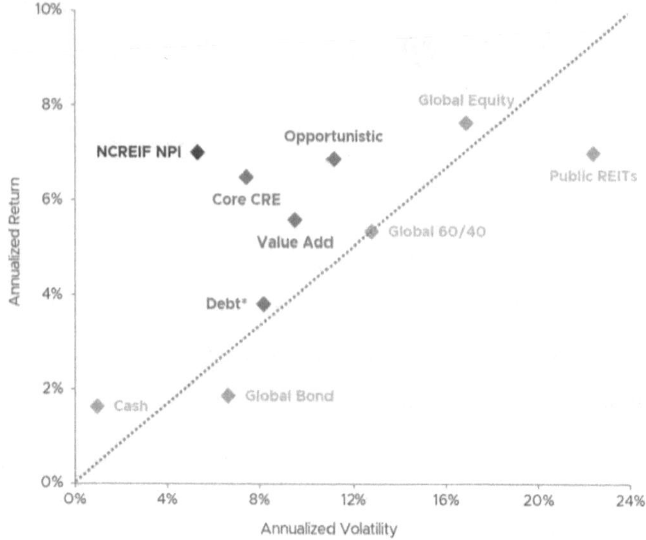

Source: iCapital

Exhibit 2: Private real estate outperforms the global 60% stock – 40% bonds portfolio

Source: iCapital

Exhibit 3: US Private Real Estate has delivered competitive long-term return potential

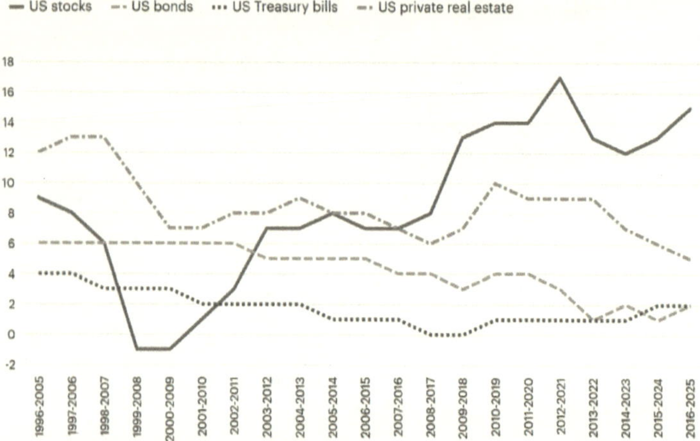

Source: Invesco Real Estate with data sourced from Bloomberg L.P., Moody's Analytics, and NCREIF. Based on quarterly annualized returns. Full period of returns ranges from Jan. 1, 1997 – Dec. 31, 2025. Stocks represented by the S&P 500 Index. Bonds represented by the Bloomberg US Aggregate Bond Index. Real estate represented by the NCREIF Property Index (NPI). T-bills represented by the 3-month US Government Treasury Bill Yield.

Exhibit 4: Real Estate Has the Least Number of Down Years - Up and Down Years for Real Estate, Stocks, And Bonds (Source: 37 Parallel Properties.com)

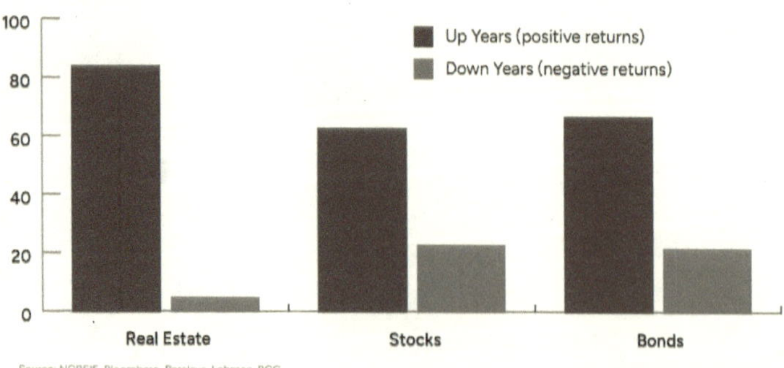

Exhibit 5: Multifamily Remains A Favorite Among CRE Asset Classes (despite recent turbulence)

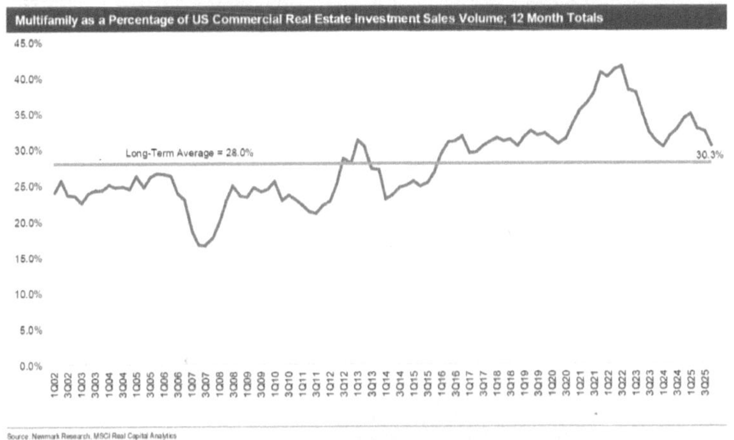

Source: Newmark

2. **Potential For Multiple Sources of Return, Including Forced Appreciation.** While there are many market factors driving apartment value, as an owner operator one has the opportunity to force appreciation by improving the profitability of a property – either through revenue growth (by raising rents or creating other sources of income) or through expense reduction (by running the property more efficiently via technology solutions or negotiating contracts to keep expenses at market or passing on some of the expenses (e.g., utility) to the tenant) or through capital improvements.

   Economies of scale are also a factor, given there are multiple units under one roof.

3. **Tax Deferral.** I discuss depreciation in more detail below (CHAPTER 26) but briefly - depreciation is the non-cash deduction one takes while owning a property, as it is presumed that the building depreciates due to age and wear and tear over time. This non-cash expense could often result in a paper loss that can either help offset current taxable income or other passive income or carry over the losses to offset future capital gains and thereby defers the tax liability. The benefit of such deferral is the time value of money. If in the end there is still a gain, there may be an opportunity to further defer such a gain into the future. As always, consult with your CPA on if and how that applies to you.
4. **Inflation Protection.** The minimum projected or target cash on cash target return for multifamily investments is 6-8% (8-10% during boom market or 4-6% during softer markets). This tracks above the current inflation rate and above returns of other asset classes. However, on top of the cash flow being generated by the property, as noted above, improving the net operating income of a property (assuming all else equal and assuming stable markets) results in improved property valuation. Over time this real estate appreciation could serve as a hedge against inflation. Other hard assets or commodities share the same benefit. In contrast, keeping cash in the bank earning 1% or less in interest over time loses value as that cash loses its purchasing power with inflation.
5. **Strong long-term outlook** due to multifamily serving a basic human need for shelter, with increasing demand driven by population growth, moderating supply (as of

the time of writing this book), declining homeownership trends (due to low affordability), and increasing share of renters (millennials and boomers).

6. **Short-term leases (typically 1 year)** allow for timely adjustment to rents based on market conditions. In contrast, other commercial real estate asset classes such as retail, office, or industrial often have multi-year leases (granted some may have built-in rent escalations).
7. **Diversified tenant base.** Each lease represents a small share of the total thereby creating less risk should one in twenty tenants leave for example. That is not to say there is no tenant sector concentration risk (e.g., if all 20 tenants in your building come from the restaurant sector for example) but one tenant leaving out of twenty is still less impactful vs. a national tenant or an anchor tenant in a 5-unit retail complex or a tenant in a single-family home leaving.

CHAPTER 4

WHY YOU SHOULD NOT INVEST IN APARTMENTS

While I love apartments, this asset class is not for everyone. As such, I think it is important to share the top 5 reasons why you might **not** want to invest in multifamily.

Higher Entry Cost. Purchasing an apartment building is not only more expensive from a purchase price perspective (vs. a single family home or a duplex), but will also require higher financing and down payment amount (typical loan to value is 60-75%, depending on the level of cash flow of the property) and upfront cash reserves (discussed in CHAPTER 17). In order to accomplish this, one needs to either raise the capital from passive investors, partner with other operators, or (in most cases) do both. Financing is also a bit more complex and has additional requirements pertaining to the property (e.g., occupancy, covenants, concentration caps, etc.) and the lead sponsor (net worth, liquidity, experience).

Asset Management Requiring Close Involvement. When one buys a property, one makes an investment. However, operating the property and managing the asset is essentially like running a business, whether you self-manage (for smaller properties) or manage the property manager. Thus, unless you invest as a limited partner (LP), you are indirectly still dealing with tenants, toilets, and trash. As with any business, you need to be abreast of the competitive landscape and market trends. Not that you do not have to be informed of such if you own other asset classes or a single family home, but it is even more important in multifamily - as you create and execute on the business plan. All of that requires a solid knowledge base and good level of experience (or at a minimum being part of an experienced team, which leads me to the next point).

Team Sport. Due to multiple aspects of the deal and its larger scale, you will need partners on your team to take deals down – acquisition (deal sourcing and broker relations, underwriting, diligence), asset management (executing on the business plan and day-to-day operations post close), and investor relations (capital raising and ongoing investor management and communications). If you are not a team player or prefer to work on your own, then that may create a challenge. Even if you take down a smaller property (16 units or less) on your own, you will eventually need a team if you want to expand and scale up further. It is also important to have a team with aligned visions/goals, complimentary skills, and strong experience level.

Regulations. This is relevant in general for any business but is particularly important, if you are syndicating multifamily investments, as you are in essence issuing securities. If you do not follow the pre-established rules of the road and the regulations, you may risk hefty fines or imprisonment. Beyond syndications, there are also leasing/tenant laws, which one needs to follow (your property management firm should be well versed in those, as they vary from city to city, county, and state).

Illiquid Investment. While this last factor pertains to real estate in general (vs. multifamily only), it is important to remember that unlike other asset classes (stocks), it may take 60-90 days or more to sell the property (or longer if the market is soft), i.e., it is not something you can liquidate overnight. In addition, if the deal was taken down as a syndication, you will have post close activities to address (e.g., tax filings and returns) and may need to keep the LLC that was created for the specific transaction active for any incidentals that may pop up post close, including tax filings.

Bonus. I recognize that I said I will share five reasons but I will add one more. Historically and relative to other CRE asset classes, given their risk profile (as seen in the charts in CHAPTER 3), apartments have not generated the highest returns. Thus, for investors who have higher risk appetite, other asset classes may be able to provide higher potential returns in exchange for higher risk (see CHAPTER 38).

If after considering these factors you still find that multifamily aligns with your goals and risk tolerance, the next question becomes how you want to participate — and for many busy professionals, the answer lies in passive investing.

CHAPTER 5

WHY PASSIVE INVESTING?

There are many advantages of investing in real estate, including monthly cash flow, appreciation & wealth creation, tax deferral benefits, diversification, and leverage, as noted previously. Thus, all you need to do is buy a property and collect the monthly cash flow, right? Not quite.

Like any other investment, purchasing real estate requires upfront diligence and managing the asset in order to optimize performance and returns. The beauty of real estate is that one can implement various investment approaches – active, passive, or a combination of both.

The **active** approach requires time, high level of commitment, and experience. As an active operator you invest time in selecting a market, building relationships with local brokers or directly with owners, finding a deal that meets the criteria of your partners and investors, vetting and selecting your deal team (property manager, attorney, CPA, lender, asset manager, contractor, etc.), managing the manager, and executing on the business plan. As an active investor, you are the hands-on owner-operator/sponsor/General Partner "GP", you carry the risk of personal liability (should a professional tenant initiate a lawsuit for example), and you may also need to put up personal liquidity and your personal balance sheet into the deal.

The **passive** approach requires capital and upfront diligence to vet the sponsor and the investment asset. Thereafter, the investors have the potential to receive monthly cash flow and are typically paid their share of the profits before the GP (if the deal performs as intended *and* if structured as such - more on that later in the book, see CHAPTERS 17, 24, and 32). As a passive investor/Limited Partner (LP), you do not control the daily operations of or make decisions on how to operate the assets (including when to sell the asset), which is why you need to be comfortable with the sponsor's character, their ability to execute, and their overall track record. However, your personal liability is also limited.

Both passive and active real estate investing can allow for the creation of cash flow. Over time, this can add up to building meaningful liquidity and a monthly income stream that can help create more optionality for you and yours.

CHAPTER 6

WHY PASSIVE INVESTING IS NOT FULLY PASSIVE

I cringe when I read how passive investing on social media is often described as sitting on a beach, sipping pina coladas, and doing no work. I suppose that is possible in theory. However, from my own experience (as both an active and a passive investor) this differs from reality. I do not want to burst your bubble. However, this myth has bothered me for some time and to a point where I think it is important to dispel a few misconceptions.

Accumulating the excess liquidity needed to invest in alternatives, like buying a business or buying real estate, for most people comes via generating active income and being fiscally responsible. In this book I have shared some of my thoughts on that topic and how to get started. This alone requires years of hard work and does not happen overnight.

After one is in a position to invest that excess cash and diversify their portfolio and after they have clarity re their investment goals and objectives (as discussed in CHAPTER 2), there are certain steps investors should take in order to minimize the risk of loss (after all, **all investments carry risk**).

It starts with **education**. Understanding the underlying asset class, how it makes money, what type of diligence is required to properly vet the asset class, market, sub-market, operator/fund manager, and the deal itself. That process takes time and requires reading multiple books and guides, connecting with fellow investors, attending industry events (like meet ups, courses, webinars, and conferences), learning how to analyze a deal, and reviewing multiple deals and offerings.

As investors, when presented with an investment opportunity, we then move to the *verify then trust stage*, where we perform the required **due diligence** on the underlying investment to determine if its risk/return profile aligns with our own investment objectives.

Even after closing on a deal, I encourage investors to **monitor their investment** via the monthly/quarterly reporting provided by the lead sponsor/fund manager, even when the distributions are flowing. This will provide you with a good perspective on the various reports, their level of detail, and the communication style of each sponsor/fund manager. In addition, this will allow you to spot any unusual trends early and ask the important questions (vs. being surprised when a capital call is executed or distributions pause).

Last but not least, managing one's investment portfolio requires **strategic tax planning**, especially when facing situations of an upcoming exit with a large gain. This is why working with a seasoned tax advisor well versed in real estate is extremely important.

I realize this message may have burst the bubble for many. However, I felt it is important to speak about the topic because after all there is no free lunch. Time, effort to get educated and follow the markets and trends, persistence, and patience are key ingredients for success in investing ...so in the end you can enjoy a little bit of time off on the beach sipping pina coladas.

PART 2

HOW SYNDICATIONS ACTUALLY WORK

CHAPTER 7

THE BENEFITS OF REAL ESTATE SYNDICATIONS FOR PASSIVE INVESTORS

For many investors, direct real estate ownership can be difficult to access. Purchasing and operating a property requires significant capital, time, experience, and operational infrastructure. Real estate syndications offer a way for investors to participate in larger institutional-quality properties while remaining largely passive.

In a syndication structure, a group of investors pools capital to acquire and operate a property. The day-to-day execution is handled by the sponsor/ operator, while passive investors participate financially in the investment.

When structured properly, syndications can offer several benefits.

Cash Flow

One of the primary attractions of multifamily syndications is the potential to generate regular income through property cash flow.

As tenants pay rent and the property generates income above operating expenses and debt service, a portion of that income is typically distributed to investors. While distributions are never guaranteed, well-structured multifamily investments often aim to provide steady income during the hold period.

For many investors, this income stream can supplement W2 income, business income, or retirement income.

Long-Term Wealth Building Through Appreciation

In addition to income, syndications also offer the potential for long-term wealth creation through appreciation.

Appreciation may occur through two primary mechanisms:

- **Operational improvements** such as increasing rents, reducing expenses, or improving property management.
- **Market-driven factors** such as population growth, job creation, and supply-demand imbalances in a given market.

When a property increases in value and is eventually sold or refinanced, investors typically participate in the upside based on their ownership share. Needless to say, whether such upside is realized in part or in full is contingent on market conditions and the execution of the business plan, i.e., never guaranteed.

Over time, however, this combination of cash flow and appreciation could contribute meaningfully to portfolio growth.

Tax Efficiency and Deferral

Real estate has long been favored by investors because of its tax characteristics.

Multifamily investments often benefit from depreciation, which may offset a portion of the income generated by the property. As a result, some or all of the cash flow distributed to investors may be tax-deferred during the hold period.

Additionally, depending on the investment structure and individual circumstances, investors may have opportunities to defer capital gains through mechanisms such as 1031 exchanges.

As always, investors should consult their tax advisors, as tax outcomes vary by individual situation.

Limited Liability and Passive Participation

Another important feature of syndications is limited liability.

Investors typically participate as limited partners in the ownership entity. This structure limits their financial liability to the amount invested, while the sponsor manages the operational responsibilities of the property.

For investors who want exposure to real estate without the burden of property management, tenant issues, financing negotiations, or construction oversight, this passive structure can be particularly attractive.

A Practical Path to Real Estate Ownership

For many investors, syndications provide access to opportunities that might otherwise be difficult to pursue individually.

Larger properties can benefit from professional management, operational scale, and institutional financing, all of which may improve the stability of the investment.

While every investment carries risk and requires careful diligence, syndications can offer a practical way to participate in real estate while maintaining a largely passive role.

Understanding how these structures work - and how to evaluate them carefully - is an important step for any investor considering multifamily investing.

CHAPTER 8

WHY YOU SHOULD NOT INVEST IN SYNDICATIONS

In an effort to present a more balanced view, I think it is important to discuss the reasons why syndications might **not** be a great fit for you.

Lack of control. When you invest passively in syndications, you join in as a Limited Partner ("LP"). As an LP you are not involved in the day-to-day operations and do not have voting power on all major decisions. In exchange, you are also shielded from business liability associated with operating the property. As such, it is important that you know and have confidence in the operator, his/her team, and their ability to execute on the business plan.

Large upfront investment. For most syndications, the minimum investment amount starts at $50,000 (most start at $100,000). And while one can invest via a self-directed IRA or Solo 401K plan (i.e., leveraging liquidity from a self-directed retirement account vs. dipping into excess liquidity sitting in a bank account or having to find additional liquidity), that is not a small amount of money for many people and may preclude some from investing.

Long-term horizon and illiquid investment. While the market environment in 2021-2022 was somewhat unusual, with many syndications selling the property within 1-3 years, the typical hold is 5-7 years. As noted above, as an LP, you do not control when the investment is sold and cannot freely sell your share. You need to be comfortable with not being able to access the invested liquidity for a period of time.

Complexity and administrative burden. As discussed previously, buying apartments entails not only making a real estate investment, but also running a business. As you do your diligence on the investment, you need to ensure you understand the market, the sub-market, the business plan and have confidence in the operator's ability to execute on such business plan by vetting such operator. The administrative burden can also be a nuisance to some – both when submitting your commitment (especially for accredited investors who go through a third-party accreditation verification process), reviewing a number of documents (e.g., Private Placement Memorandum, Investment Summary, deal underwrite, etc.), tracking portfolio performance over time, as well as working through the annual tax reporting (e.g., annual K1 reporting for taxes).

Small ownership share. While typical ownership share splits grant approximately 70% ownership share to the passive investors (LPs), that 70% share is distributed among several individuals/entities. In addition, the deal sponsors (managing partners) will often establish caps on the maximum permissible investment amount. This, in turn, limits your ownership share and ability to control the deal. While a small share of a big pie can still be quite meaningful to an investor, it caps the share of profits you capture.

Other: In the current market environment, particularly in the first year of operations while the sponsors are stabilizing the property, cash flow is limited. While as an LP you mostly benefit from the ongoing preferred return (think of it as interest paid on the principal amount you invested in the deal, though it is NOT exactly the same especially for tax purposes), the preferred return is not guaranteed. Thus, the biggest potential gain for both LPs and the GPs (deal sponsors) is generated at the time of sale, timing of which depends on the hold period (i.e., is not immediate). If you invest a small principal amount, that might equate to a relatively small amount of monthly income (though as shared in CHAPTER 42, that can stack up over time in a meaningful way).

3 Myths On (Real Estate) Investing

In my experience as both an active and passive investor I have encountered three common but dangerous beliefs passive investors often have. Some I learned through hardship (a loss on one of my own passive deals, thankfully relatively early in my journey) and others I see often floating around.

As it has been my mission to create empowered and educated passive investors by sharing my experience, knowhow, and lessons learned, I feel it is important to speak about these misconceptions. I realize this is a sensitive topic and I may get a lot of heat for what I am about to share. But I am ok with that, as I am speaking my truth and the benefit of shedding light on some hidden nuances exceeds the cost of the criticism this post may raise.

1. **Wide social media presence of the lead sponsor/ syndicators.** While it is important that the lead sponsor is out there and known to the public, this should never be one of your key criteria when selecting one. Some syndicators in the space are very strong at marketing but do not necessarily have the finance and/or operational expertise to do proper diligence, operations, and monitoring of the investment.

   Later in this book (CHAPTER 21), I share key questions to ask the lead sponsors, how to vet their track record, how to find them. It is also imperative that investors perform deep diligence via professional background checks. You can find a detailed sponsor vetting checklist here: www.dbacapitalgroup.com/book-resources .

2. **Guaranteed returns.** There is no such thing as a guaranteed return because all investments carry risk, including the risk for a total loss. Even Treasuries carry risk. After all, projections are exactly that – projections, i.e., the pro forma numbers you see will never exactly match the actual delivered post close. They will be higher or lower.

   Often passive investors think (or some sponsors represent) that preferred returns are guaranteed. This is far from the truth. Even though preferred returns rank higher in the cash flow waterfall, this does not mean that they will be paid out, especially if the deal fails or underperforms.

I also often see debt funds being presented as guaranteed or secure forms of returns. As a former commercial lender, this statement makes me cringe as it implies the probability of loan loss is zero...Take a look at any bank's financials and show me where they show zero allowances for loan losses...

3. **High risk = high returns.** High risk **does not** equal high return but rather equals a high probability for loss. As such, it is important to understand: (i) the risk profile of a deal (I have previously posted the 10-part video series on understanding the key risks when underwriting multifamily deals, which you can find on my YouTube channel https://www.youtube.com/@DreamBelieveAchieveRealEstate), (ii) the risk mitigates, and (iii) whether or not such risk profile aligns with your own risk tolerance and target risk-adjusted expected returns. You should be compensated for taking on higher risk but that alone should not be a reason to take on more risk.

I said my piece and hope this helps shed some light on a few common misconceptions, so you can dig deeper next time you encounter one or some of those and hopefully make more informed investment decisions as a result.

CHAPTER 9

506B AND 506C STRUCTURES

It all began almost 100 years ago with tracts of citrus groves in sunny Florida and W. J. Howey Co ("Howey"). Howey sold tracts of citrus groves to buyers in Florida, who would then lease back the land to Howey. Howey would tend to the groves and harvest, pool, and market the produce on behalf of the owners. Both parties shared in the revenue. Most buyers had no experience, knowledge, skills, or equipment needed in agriculture and were not involved in the day-to-day operations themselves.

What Howey had failed to do was register the transactions with the U.S. Securities and Exchange Commission (SEC) and so the SEC intervened in 1946. The court›s final ruling determined the leaseback arrangements qualified as investment contracts.

The case resulted in a test, known as the Howey test, a four-prong test used to determine whether an instrument qualifies as an "investment contract" for the purposes of the Securities Act: "a contract, transaction or scheme whereby a person (1) invests his/her money (2) in a common enterprise and (3) with the expectation of profits (4) generated solely from the efforts of the promoter or a third party."

That is how syndications were born. For a long time, however, investments in syndications were limited for the super wealthy... until 2012 when the Jumpstart Our Business Startups Act, or JOBS Act, among other things, reduced barriers to capital formation, particularly for smaller companies. The JOBS Act requires the SEC to adopt rules amending existing exemptions from registration under the Securities Act of 1933 and creating new exemptions that permit issuers of securities to raise capital without SEC registration, which registration is not only costly and document intensive, but also takes a long time. In 2013, the SEC adopted amendments to Rule 506 of Regulation D and Rule 144A under the Securities Act to implement the requirements of Section 201(a) of the JOBS Act. Those exemptions, while applicable to business in general, were also beneficial for the real estate industry overall as they opened opportunities for the average person to participate in large real estate investments.

The two most common SEC exemptions are Rule 506 (B) and Rule 506 (C). They represent private offerings that are regulated differently from public ones (e.g., stocks).

506 (B)

Under Rule 506 (B), a sponsor can raise an unlimited amount of capital from unlimited number of accredited investors and up to 35 non-accredited but sophisticated investors.

The full SEC definition of **accredited investor** (https://www.sec.gov/resources-small-businesses/exempt-offerings/frequently-asked-questions-about-exempt-offerings) is more comprehensive. However, as it applies to individuals investing in syndications it captures either individuals making **at least**

$200,000 in gross annual income in each of the two most recent years (or joint income, with a spouse or partner, exceeding $300,000) or individuals with **net worth (individual or joint) exceeding $1,000,000, excluding the person's (couple's) primary residence**. There have been recent discussions of increasing the minimum income base and net worth base and implementing the option for sophisticated investors to take an exam to achieve accredited investor status. As of the time of writing this book, this new regulation is not in effect.

The full SEC definition includes a few more qualifying categories that allow one to certify as an accredited investor:

- an SEC-registered broker-dealer, SEC- or state-registered investment adviser, or exempt reporting adviser
- a director, executive officer, or general partner of the company selling the securities, or any director, executive officer, or general partner of a general partner of that company
- a trust with assets exceeding $5 million, not formed only to acquire the securities offered, and whose purchases are directed by a person who meets the legal standard of having sufficient knowledge and experience in financial and business matters to be capable of evaluating the merits and risks of the prospective investment
- an entity of a type not otherwise qualifying as accredited that own investments in excess of $5 million
- an individual holding in good standing any of the general securities representative license (Series 7), the investment adviser representative license (Series 65),

or the private securities offerings representative license (Series 82)

- a knowledgeable employee, as defined in rule 3c-5(a)(4) under the Investment Company Act, of the issuer of securities where that issuer is a 3(c)(1) or 3(c)(7) private fund or
- a family office and its family clients if the family office has assets under management in excess of $5 million and whose prospective investments are directed by a person who has such knowledge and experience in financial and business matters that such family office is capable of evaluating the merits and risks of the prospective investment

A **sophisticated investor** does not meet the income or net worth hurdles of an accredited investor noted above; however, possesses business/finance/investment knowledge and experience to properly evaluate the risks and benefits of the investment.

Under the 506 (B) exemption, the sponsor is **<u>not</u>** allowed to solicit or to publicly advertise the offering, including via social media or e-mail blasts. The sponsor is only allowed to share the offering with individuals/entities they have a substantive pre-existing relationship with. Such substantive relationship is usually established over time.

When participating in a 506 (B) offering, investors self-certify their accreditation status.

506 (C)

Under Rule 506 (C), a sponsor can raise an unlimited amount of capital from unlimited number of accredited investors.

The sponsor is allowed to publicly advertise the offering and a pre-existing substantive relationship is not a requirement (but recommended).

When participating in a 506 (C) offering, investors undergo a third party written verification process to validate their accreditation status. Such third-party validation may also be performed by the investor's CPA or investment advisor.

An SEC **qualified client** is an investor eligible to pay performance-based fees to investment advisers under Investment Advisers Act Rule 205-3. As of 2021, they must meet at least one of these thresholds: **$1,100,000 in Assets Under Management (AUM)** with the adviser, or a **net worth over $2,200,000** (excluding primary residence). Such net worth requirement is adjusted periodically based on inflation (the next adjustment is expected in June 2026).

A question that I am often asked is – how can one become an accredited investor, if one cannot meet the requirements above?

Many individuals opt in to take the Series 65 exam and license as it also enables them to earn income as investment advisers. Taking the exam entails 20-40 hours of studying, a small $200 or so fee, and a passing grade of 80%. Thereafter one does not lose the license as long as one continues to work for a sponsoring firm in the financial services industry. If you leave your sponsoring employer, you must find a new sponsor within two years to keep your license current. There are third party firms like Regdee (regdee.com) that offer not only help with the testing and registration process, but also with compliance and license maintenance for a small annual fee.

In addition, as of May 2023, the House voted to pass legislation, administering the SEC to introduce an exam program that would qualify investors as accredited. The accredited investor exam would require potential investors to demonstrate a certain level of financial sophistication and understanding of investment concepts. As of the time of this writing, this is not yet law.

Thus, there are a few more options beyond the income and net worth traditional accreditation requirements that open up a world of investment opportunities and we thought it is important to share some of the nuances of the definition as well as alternative options to achieve accreditation status.

The rules and laws regulating the 506 (B) and 506 (C) offering have many more requirements that a sponsor is/should be well aware of and adhere to. However, herein I am only sharing the ones that passive investors more commonly come across. I recognize this content is denser as usual. Nevertheless, I thought it was important to share and hope you found it helpful.

CHAPTER 10

WHAT TO EXPECT BEFORE, DURING, AND AFTER A SYNDICATION

A question I am frequently asked from passive investors (LPs) pertains to the process of a real estate syndication. I discuss how to evaluate the sponsorship team (CHAPTER 21), the market (CHAPTER 15), property types (CHAPTER 16), and the deal structure/underwrite (CHAPTER 17) as well as the different syndication structures (CHAPTERs 12, 13, and 24). Below I will provide a step-by-step overview of the syndication process and what to expect at each stage.

The Syndication Investment Process:

1. The sponsor announces that they have a deal. In that announcement (typically sent via e-mail or text), the sponsor will also invite you to the investor presentation.
    - If the offering is a 506 (C), the sponsor may advertise that publicly.
    - If the offering is 506 (B), the sponsor would share the deal only with investors whom they have a pre-existing substantive relationship with.

2. The sponsor conducts the investor presentation webinar, which is typically recorded. This is your opportunity to ask your initial questions to determine if this is a deal you want to invest in. You should feel free to address follow up questions directly to the sponsor you have a relationship with after the presentation too.
3. The sponsor will send a call recording along with a link to the investment portal, where you can also access the investment documents – PPM (private placement memorandum), the investment offering, and the operating agreement, investor questionnaire, and wire instructions.
4. Read and understand the PPM and ancillary documents. This is your opportunity to ask follow up questions to ensure you are comfortable with the management team, the market, the key underwriting assumptions, and deal structure.
5. You review the investment offering presentation and offering documents, and after further diligence on the sponsor, the market, and the deal, decide to invest.
6. You submit your soft commitment via the investment portal, specifying your investment amount.
    - Real estate syndications are almost always filled on a first-come, first-served basis. As such, if you want a guaranteed spot in the deal, you should wire the proceeds as soon as you feel ready to invest. Never feel pressured to do so, however – there will always be a next deal.
7. Execute the subscription agreement, complete and submit the investor questionnaire and W-9 form.

For 506 (C) structures, you will need to submit additional information, which is used to verify your accredited investor status. Typically, the accreditation verification is completed by a third party.

8. After signing the PPM, you wire in your funds.
9. The sponsor confirms that your funds and executed documents have been received.
10. The sponsor notifies you once the deal closes and next steps.

You should be receiving frequent updates between the time of wiring your funds/executing the PPM and the deal closing, which typically takes place within 45-60 days of the investor presentation.

11. The sponsor provides periodic updates and reports post close (usually monthly or quarterly financial updates). The updates are sent via e-mail. The monthly/quarterly financials and annual K-1 reports are also posted on the investor or alternate secure portal. The K-1 statements are typically due by March 15th (however, it is not uncommon for reporting to be delayed from time to time).
12. You start receiving distributions (monthly or quarterly), <u>if the deal is performing on track</u>. Some distributions start immediately and some may start at a later point in time, as determined by the sponsor and as documented in the offering documents (which is usually shared upfront).
13. The sponsor executes on the business plan, sells the asset, and you receive your share of the profits and capital gain. (It is important to note that this assumes that the deal

performed as expected. As with any investment, however, there is a possibility of partial or total loss of capital, if the investment does not perform as originally expected.)

14. Rinse and repeat as you continue to build your passive income portfolio.

CHAPTER 11

UNDERSTANDING KEY TERMS

NOI = Net Operating Income

In more simplified terms, NOI equals Revenues minus Operating Expenses and represents the operating profit generated by the property before debt service, capex, or other extraordinary items. As such, the two key components of NOI are revenue and expenses.

- The Revenue line item represents the sum of total rental income generated by the property plus other income (e.g., pet fees, laundry fees, valet trash fees, utility reimbursements, other fees, etc.). More often than not, when you review the operating statements of a property you will see that expressed on a gross basis as total scheduled rental income with vacancy and other reserves (bad debt, concessions, other reserves, etc.) factored in as separate line items to arrive at net rental revenue. You will often hear that referred to as **effective gross income**.
- The Expense line item captures all operating expenses related to the property, which typically include but are not limited to property taxes, property management fees, insurance, repair and maintenance, utilities (if landlord

paid), contract services (e.g., pest control, landscaping, etc.), general and admin expenses, replacement reserves, etc. Typically operating expenses are 50% of the effective gross income discussed above. However, the expense ratio may vary based on the property type/age/location. For example: (i) it is not uncommon for larger properties to operate at 40-45% expense ratio based on economies of scale or (ii) to see a 30% expense ratio for properties in Denver, CO or Phoenix, AZ (due to lower tax and insurance expenses).

Physical Vacancy: reflects actual units vacant

Economic Vacancy: adjusts for additional factors such as collections, bad debt, concessions, units reserved for staff, etc., essentially how much one actually collects

Break Even Occupancy – unit count and %

As the name of this Key Performance Indicator (KPI) may imply, it measures at what point of occupancy does revenue generated by the property cover the property expenses (including debt service) just enough to break even. It is calculated as total operating expenses plus debt service divided by gross potential rental income. A break even of 80% simply means that GROSS income can decline by 20% before the property breaks even. A break even of 70% or less is generally considered acceptable. Any number larger than 80% implies there is very little room for error in case of potential deterioration. As a reference point, agency lenders would often have a 90% physical occupancy minimum.

Modified Break Even: This KPI is similar to Break-Even Occupancy, except that the sum of total operating expenses and debt service is divided by gross effective income. As such, it indicates how much income (which may include other income streams beyond rent and also captures economic and physical vacancy) can fall before the property breaks even. This metric is often more favored by lenders and a bit more conservative (it is also the one I use). A break even ratio of 80% would indicate NET revenues could drop by 20% before the property reaches a break even profit level.

DSC = Debt Service Coverage

DSC equals the NOI divided by the principal and interest debt service. Effectively it measures ability of the cash flow generated by the property (NOI) to service the debt (debt service). Most often lenders would require a min of 1.25x DSC, though this number can range from as low as 1.10x to as high as 1.35x. As an operator, you want to have some cushion. I typically want to see a DSC min of 1.4-1.6x. And in a worst case scenario, you do not want DSC to fall below 1.0x, which simply means the property does not generate enough cash flow to cover the minimum debt obligation. If that occurs, the owners would be required to cover the deficit (or take other action to cure the bank covenant default).

Reserves

Simply put, this is your rainy day bucket. Good practice would be to set aside 6-12 months of reserves. It is also not uncommon for the lender to establish what these reserve minimums are. However, whether mandated by the lender or not, one should always set aside reserves upfront (in addition to the replacement reserves captured in the p&l) as unexpected expenses will and do happen.

Key Return Metrics Fundamentals

I am often asked – how do you measure performance of your real estate asset? While there are numerous key performance indicators used to assess asset performance, below I will focus on key return metrics that you will often come across when speaking with sponsors and reviewing various deal investment opportunities.

Cash on Cash Return (CoC) = cash income earned relative to the original cash investment. The original cash investment typically includes the down payment on a loan (if the property is financed), closing costs, capex reserves, and operating reserves. For example, a property generating $10,000 in annual cash flow after debt service and initial cash investment of $100,000, has a 10% cash on cash return.

A typical minimum potential CoC target for syndicated investments is 4-10% (4-6% in softer markets and 8-10% in strong markets). It is not uncommon for the cash-on-cash return to be lower in years 1-2, while the property is being stabilized.

Average Annual Return (AAR) = return **on** investment *averaged over the hold period of the asset*, measured as total distribution to members <u>divided by</u> the initial cost of the investment or cash investment. The total distribution to member is equal to cash flow from operations and the gain at the time of sale. If the asset is refinanced, thereby returning a portion or all of the initial equity investment, this metric is less meaningful and, in that scenario, it is generally better to refer to the Internal Rate of Return.

A typical minimum AAR target for syndicated investments is 13-15%. It is not uncommon for the average return to be lower in years 1-2, while the property is being stabilized.

Internal Rate of Return (IRR) = this metric captures the full return **on** the investment including distribution to members (referenced above) coupled with the gain on sale after **accounting for time value of money**. The timing of when cash flow is returned impacts the IRR. Therefore, the sooner you receive the cash back, i.e., the shorter the hold period, the higher the IRR. This metric is less relevant for long-term buy and hold JV deals (cash on cash return would be a better return gauge for those long-term buys and holds).

IRR target minimum for syndicated apartment investments is 15-22% (13-15% in softer markets).

Equity Multiple (EM) = measured as total dollars received divided by total dollars invested. Total dollars received includes the cash flow earned throughout the hold period of the asset coupled with the sale proceeds. For example, if you invested $100,000 and you received a total of $200,000 throughout the hold period of the asset including gain on sale, that means you achieved equity multiple of 2.00x or in other words you doubled your initial investment.

A typical minimum potential EM target for syndicated investments is 1.40-2.00x over a 5-year period (lower in softer markets).

Return On Equity (ROE) = Total Annual Return (Cash Flow + Principal Paydown + Appreciation) / Total Equity or in other words the net profit derived from the investment divided by the initial equity. Total Equity captures the initial investment (down payment and closing costs). Equity is a measure of how much of your net worth you have tied up in a property, and the amount of cash you would have in the bank if you sold it today (after paying off the debt on the property).

Cap Rate Fundamentals

In simple terms, the cap rate (aka the capitalization rate) represents the rate of return on a real estate investment property based on the income such property generates/is expected to generate.

Cap Rate = Net Operating Income / Property Purchase Price

Conversely, if one has the Net Operating Income generated by the property and the market cap rate, one can back into the potential valuation of the property.

Some people refer to cap rate as the unlevered rate of return, as it is based on net operating income (vs. cash flow after debt service). Others refer to it as the inverse of the price-earnings multiple.

The cap rate can be affected by a number of factors – underlying economic or market fundamentals, interest rates, demand for and supply of the underlying asset, asset class, location, building age and condition, etc. For example, an older property located in a tertiary market is likely to have a higher cap rate vs. a newer property located in a secondary market. A multifamily (apartment building) property will have a different (usually lower) cap rate relative to hotels or office buildings. In a competitive market environment where demand exceeds supply (like the market conditions in 2021-2022), increasing competition and hence higher prices will further drive cap rates down.

Usually, the higher the risk profile of the asset, the higher the expected cap rate will be.

If one thinks as the 10-year Treasury as being the risk-free rate of return, the difference between the cap rate and the Treasury rate (aka the spread) will reflect the risk premium one receives for investing in the subject asset class. In an effort to predict cap rates, many would usually observe the 10-year Treasury. As a point of reference, the long-term average spread for apartments is approx. 150-200 bps (1.5-2.00%), i.e., cap rates should track 150-200bps higher than the 10-year Treasury.

With that said, data suggests that the relationship between the 10-year US Treasury rate and cap rates is not necessarily correlated (I will let my statistician friends go through the exercise of proving that empirically). While usually cap rates may trend upward as interest rates rise, that rise does not always occur at the same pace. In addition, a period of rising interest rates does not necessarily mean cap rates will increase. For example, if real estate as an asset class remains preferable due to growth or inflation expectations or due to its better risk profile relative to other alternatives, then the spread can compress instead.

Another point of comparison that some people observe is that between the cap rate and the loan interest rate. If the cap rate is lower than the loan interest rate (aka negative leverage), it should put you on notice to be careful of overleverage and whether you should even lever the property.

During the 2020-2022 boom, as competition for properties was increasing and bid prices up, we observed further cap rate compression. In addition, cap rate spread compression was observed among asset types (Class A vs. Class B vs. Class C), leading operators at that time to purchase Class C assets at nearly Class A cap rates (we will cover asset class definitions in CHAPTER 16).

As you evaluate a property's projected performance, pay special attention to the cap rate assumptions. While no one has a crystal ball to predict exactly where cap rates will be 3-5-7 years from now, even a few basis points difference in cap rates, can make a meaningful impact on a property's valuation. Thus, you should understand what cap rate assumptions a sponsor is applying as they perform property proforma valuations, which ultimately also factor into return fundamentals such as IRR. It is prudent for a more conservative operator to assume a 10-15 bps cap rate increase annually throughout the projection period.

I know this was a lot to digest, so I shall stop here. I hope you found the above overview helpful and now feel better equipped with yet another tool (metric) to evaluate properties. And if you want to have some fun, mention cap rates next time you speak with commercial real estate investors and you can look forward to an engaging conversation with multitude of views and opinions.

CHAPTER 12

UNDERSTANDING THE FEES IN A SYNDICATION

Below I will demystify the fees you may encounter in a real estate syndication. Not all of them would apply to an investment opportunity. Nevertheless, it may be helpful to be aware of most.

Acquisition Fee (2-5% of purchase price, 3% being typical and anything higher being exorbitant unless the property value is super small) - typically paid to the General Partners (GPs) at close. However, in some scenarios, some GPs may choose to invest the proceeds in the deal or may delay collection of the fee until a certain Limited Partner (LP) return is achieved. GPs would often review many deals before they find the one where the numbers make sense. This process will often entail additional expense, such as travel, earnest money deposits gone hard on a deal they ultimately chose to walk away from, diligence reports/reviews on a deal that did not move forward, etc. The acquisition fee partially compensates GPs for that effort and the aforementioned out of pocket costs.

Asset Management Fee (1-2% of net operating income) - typically paid out of the monthly cash flow. It compensates the GP for the time and effort involved in actively managing the asset to ensure execution against the original business plan progresses as scheduled. It is imperative to understand how the asset management fee is calculated as in rare instances, some operators base it on the equity amount raised for single asset syndications. While this is not an uncommon approach for funds (more on that in CHAPTER 25), for a single asset syndication this is an indicator of misaligned incentives. For me personally, this is a hard NO but I understand every investor has their own criteria on what is acceptable or not.

Construction Management Fee (5% of the rehab budget) – for properties that may require more work to turn around in a short period of time, it serves to compensate the GP during that transition period for managing contractors, leasing efforts, and the property manager. It is important that the fee is only collected if the project performs on time and on budget. If performance triggers are not built in, this is a red flag indicating misalignment of incentives.

Refinance Fee (1-2% of loan amount) – typically paid at close of the refinance (refi). It compensates the GP for managing the loan refi process, which would include soliciting proposals, evaluating and selecting the optimal refi terms, working with the lender and property manager to provide the needed information to complete the refi, and coordinating post close activities related to return of capital to the LPs.

Loan Broker Fee (1-2% of loan amount) – typically paid at close and designed to compensate the mortgage broker for the work put in to solicit the best financing terms and position the deal for success to the ultimate lender. This is a pass through fee, i.e., not a fee the GP team would collect.

Guarantor Fee (1-2% of purchase price) - typically paid at close and designed to compensate the guarantor for putting up their personal balance sheet behind the deal. It is usually added when the guarantor (key principal) is not part of the core GP team. The guarantor may or may not be involved in the day-to-day operations (though they should as they are putting their personal name, credit, and balance sheet on the line). Therefore, they would want to be extra comfortable with the operators' ability to execute before signing the dotted line with their name. If the deal was to go bad, their name would be on the line.

Disposition Fee (1-2% of sale price) - typically paid at close/sale. It compensates the GP for the work put into preparing the property for sale and coordinating the sale to completion. If a disposition fee is charged, then the acquisition fee is in most cases no more than 2%.

CHAPTER 13

UNDERSTANDING DIFFERENT DISTRIBUTION TYPES AND WATERFALL STRUCTURES

As noted in the preceding sections, distributions are how investors and operators get paid during the life of a deal before the gain from sale arrives. Understanding the timing of distributions is important as previously noted, and so is the structure of such distributions.

So long as the property generates sufficient cash flow, typically the distribution is comprised of the preferred return as well as the pro rata profit share. The preferred return, as the name implies, shows preference of the LPs ahead of the GPs. It is paid first, before the pro rata share of profits is distributed.

Preferred returns are not guaranteed and depend on the cash flow generated by the property. As such, it is important to understand how they are treated in the event there is a shortfall.

The most typical structure is **cumulative**, i.e., the preferred balance due carries over into the next year. LPs may not receive the return as planned but will not lose it (unless the overall investment suffers a loss). If it keeps accumulating till sale (or another capital event such as refinance), such cumulative preferred return accrued to the LPs will typically be paid first, followed by the LP's principal investment and LP's share of the gains, and lastly the GP's share of the gain.

Cumulative and compounding is another method, whereby the preferred return not only accumulates over time, but the rate is calculated on the accrued balance (vs. the original principal balance). This method is less common and certainly more beneficial for the LPs.

In rare occasions, the preferred return may not accrue, which is the least LP-friendly structure.

Preferred return may be **calculated on returned or unreturned capital contribution principal amount**. This is why it is important to understand whether distributions constitute return on capital (most common) or return of capital (less common). Basing distributions on unreturned capital is most common and more beneficial for LPs. If distributions count towards return of the principal investment balance, then the preferred rate is based on the decreasing balance, and as such, those monthly (or quarterly) cash flows diminish over time.

It is just as important to understand the **cash flow waterfall**. In most deals, a simple waterfall structure like 70% LP and 30% GP, first distributes the preferred return, then the profits on a pro rata ownership share. However, in some deal structures, the profit share may change after a certain IRR hurdle or AAR hurdle is met. An example of such would be, 8% preferred return and 70% LP-30% GP profit share paid until sponsor hits an IRR of 15%, at which point profit split changes to 50% LP-50% GP.

There could be multiple tiers/IRR hurdles built in, typically increasing the sponsor's share of the profits.

Lastly, syndicated deals also have a **capital event waterfall.** This waterfall specifies how the proceeds would flow after a capital event such as refinance or sale. Typically, the loan and transaction fees associated with the sale would be paid first, followed by any accrued but unpaid preferred return, the LP principal, and lastly the profit split.

Note: The transaction fees would also include any GP fees, such as disposition fees. While that may be ok, if the investment meets or exceeds projections, it may become problematic if the deal underperforms or forecloses. Hopefully, if that is the case the GP would step in and share that fee with LPs to minimize the amount of principal lost.

The devil is in the details. As such, it is important to understand the distributions timing and structure upfront, so you have clear expectations on timing of cash flows and avoid surprises over the lifecycle of a deal.

CHAPTER 14

VALUE ADD INVESTING DEMYSTIFIED

When attending commercial real estate events or speaking to multifamily investors one may often hear the term "value add". What does that really mean and how does it impact the property, business plan, and investment performance over time?

In simple terms, as the name implies, the value-add approach identifies ways to add value to the property with the goal of improving cash flow and capital appreciation in an effort to achieve the property's full potential value.

Such value add can take the form of (i) **operational enhancements** such as *growing revenues* by increasing rents (e.g., bringing rents to market), *creating additional income streams* (e.g., pet fees), or *optimizing expenses* (e.g., leveraging economies of scale, implementing smart tech to reduce expenses); (ii) **capital improvements** (e.g., updating interiors or catching up to deferred maintenance), or (iii) **total repositioning** (aka heavy value add, which usually combines operational and heavy capital improvements often making the property appealing to a more affluent tenant base).

When it comes to capital improvements, evaluating the project's ROI is important when making a decision on how much and what types of investment to make in the property. Underinvesting in upgrades can leave potential revenue increases or expense reductions on the table, while overspending on improvements that do not materially increase revenue or reduce expenses can dilute returns.

Keeping the potential value at exit (aka as reversion value) is also important. More specifically, while upgrading 100 percent of the units might maximize potential revenues, doing so may completely exhaust the asset's upside potential thereby leaving no (or nearly none) value add for a potential buyer (often referred to in the industry as "leaving meat on the bone").

Value add strategies can take different forms – light value add or heavy value add. **Light value add** (aka stable value add) would revolve around operational improvements and/or minor capital improvements. **Heavy value add** (aka as major repositioning) would involve heavy capital improvements (e.g., renovating the property to the studs, implementing heavy exterior updates, etc.).

By maximizing the property's full potential value, the value-add strategy improves the property (and the area) and achieves what is known as forced appreciation. Such forced appreciation can serve as a hedge against market fluctuations. Let's see how that can actually play in practice.

For example, let's assume you purchase a 50-unit property that historically generates annual NOI of $100,000. And let's assume market cap rate at that point of time is 5.00%, yielding property value of $2MM (= $100,000 NOI / 5% cap rate).

Let's assume that through operational improvements you increase NOI by $50/unit/mo and that there are no incremental expenses associated with such NOI. This small increase would equate to a $30,000 improvement in NOI ($50 x 12 months x 50 units).

Assuming no change in market, you just increased the property value by $600K to $2.6MM (see calculation below).

Now what if the market contracts or there is a downturn and market cap rates increase from 5% to 6%. Your operational/NOI improvements yield a value of $2.16MM vs. $1.67MM if you sat and did nothing.

Exhibit 6:

	current NOI		value add NOI	
	$ 100,000	$ 100,000	$ 130,000	$ 130,000
cap rate	5%	6%	5%	6%
value	$ 2,000,000	$ 1,666,667	$2,600,000	$2,166,667

Successful implementation of the value-add model comes with its own risks and hurdles such as the risk of poor execution, the need for a high level of coordination (knowing the market, being creative, communicating with partners and vendors), upfront budgeting with a high degree of accuracy. Being slightly off budget may call for tough decisions such as modifying the initially planned updates or even worse – a capital call from the management team (GPs) or passive investors (LPs). A hot market can often hide such deficiencies or poor execution - as Warren Buffet once said: once the tide goes down, you will know who was swimming without a bathing suit.

Investment in multifamily and uncovering the property's untapped potential takes market knowledge, creativity, and strategic discipline. If used right and with proper planning and diligence, the value-add strategy can be a powerful tool allowing one to focus on what one can control by improving the property and local communities, while delivering strong returns to investors and hedging against market fluctuations (that are often outside of one's control).

PART 3

HOW TO EVALUATE DEALS

CHAPTER 15

SELECTING A MARKET

I am often asked how and why I selected the markets I invest in. There are numerous factors that go into the decision-making process. I will first focus on the key factors in selecting a market, will then offer a few other factors for your consideration, and lastly will cover a couple more metrics one should keep in mind as you narrow down the search to particular neighborhoods. In the end, I have also enclosed a sample key performance indicators (KPI) market summary of Orlando, FL.

As a passive investor you do not have to be an expert on the market or perform deep market analysis, unless you want to. It is the sponsor's job to perform the diligence and provide ongoing monitoring and their investment offering will usually have a ton of data on the city and state. However, you should at least perform a high-level diligence (trust but verify), so you are better positioned to ask questions and assess the projection assumptions used to derive proforma returns. After all, the market forms the inputs the drive the outputs for proforma returns.

A market vetting checklist and GPT is also included in the book resources page (www.dbacapitalgroup.com/book-resources).

Top 10 Key Performance Indicators (KPIs):

Population growth - at least positive but ideally 1% each year (over a period of 20 years that could represent in excess of 20% growth) or higher than overall US population growth. For smaller cities (under 250K in population) the expected growth rate should be larger (as you start from a lower base) and conversely for larger cities with a higher population base (1MM+) the expected growth rate will slow down (as you start from a higher base). Population growth matters as it ultimately drives household formation, which in turn results in demand for more housing (people need a place to live) and provides for a steady stream of customers (potential renters).

Job growth - 2% or more year over year or at least exceeding the national average. Job growth matters as it not only brings more people to the area but also provides a steady stream of income for your tenants.

Low Unemployment - at or below the national average. Similar to job growth, a low unemployment rate indicates a happily (or not so happily) employed tenants who generate at least some level of income to cover basic living expenses, including rent.

Median household income - as of the time of writing this book, the minimum I target is $50K. However, that number should adjust over time along with inflation. In addition, the median (vs. average) number is preferred as it removes any outliers.

Median household income growth - at least 1-2% per year or at a minimum exceeding rent growth for that market. While employment indicates a tenant receives a stream of earned income, this KPI measures the growth in such income and hence ability to absorb rent increases or ability to afford a more expensive asset class.

Job Diversity - diversity of industries, employers, and recession-proof companies (e.g., finance, IT, healthcare). You do not want to invest in one-horse town dominated by a single employer or two and run the risk of that firm leaving town or closing shop, thereby resulting in a ghost town and no renters.

Crime rate – under 500 of the national index and generally declining. It goes without saying that people want to feel safe at home or be able to take furry Fido for a walk safely. Crime rate not only impacts the demand for apartments but also the potential value of your property. Even the best-looking property (visually or on paper) will have a hard time selling in a crime infested area.

Regulatory environment – I generally like to invest in business friendly and landlord friendly states.

House value growth – 2% year over year. House value growth would indicate overall property appreciation. In addition, a higher home price point suggests buying a home becomes less affordable thereby pushing people to continue to rent or to upsize/upgrade instead to a nicer rental property.

Cost to Rent vs. Cost to Own Differential – measures the cost of a monthly mortgage (though home ownership inherently comes with additional expenses around insurance, maintenance, and if applicable HOA) vs. the cost to rent. Historically that number has averaged $400/mo; however, as of the time of writing this book it is approx. $1,200/mo.

Rent growth – 2% or more year over year. Rent growth naturally results in higher rent revenue and all else equal in higher operating profit for your property. We saw unprecedented (double digit) rent growth in 2021-2022. This double-digit growth rate is not sustainable in the long run unless wage growth keeps up pace (which it did not) and due to oversupply in certain markets, we subsequently saw growth soften reaching negative levels in certain markets.

Rent to Income Ratio – 30% or less (I prefer 20-25% as that number covers other fixed costs renters would incur such as taxes, insurance, food, and utilities). This KPI is an indicator of affordability. Also, a gap between current household income and median rent suggests there is further room for growth in rent before affordability becomes a constraint to rent growth.

Other KPIs:

Rent to Own Ratio – generally over 50% suggests a larger renter (vs. homeowner) base.

Supply and demand/absorption rate - the rate at which available apartments are rented in a specific market during a given time period (homes rented divided by homes available for rent over a certain period). It reveals the demand for a property or the market trend.

Other – net migration, commute time to nearby cities, walkability score, national or regional rankings, proximity to shops/retail, cost to rent vs. own, U-Haul migration trends.

Additional Neighborhood KPIs:

Poverty Rate – no higher than 15-20%. This metric ties to the affordability, ability to raise rents, crime, and overall state of the neighborhood.

Unemployment rate spread vs. the city – no more than 2% over the city unemployment rate.

Income growth outpacing home value growth – an indicator of the path of progress.

Exhibit 7: Sample KPI Summary (2021 Q4)

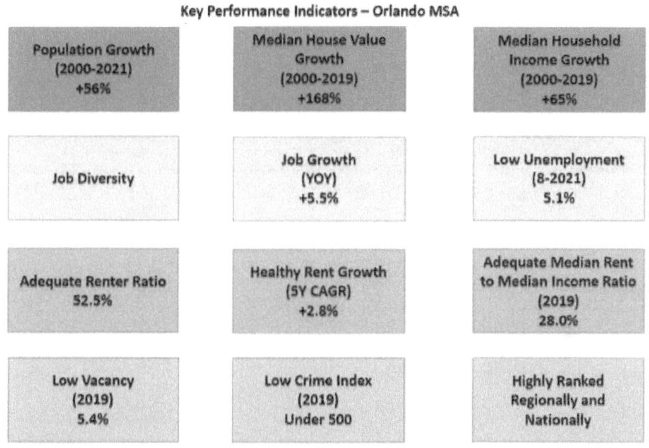

Exhibit 8: Sample KPI Summary (2026 Q1)

Key Performance Indicators

Population Growth (2000-2026) +82.7%	Median House Value Growth (2000-2025) +395%	Median Household Income Growth (2000-2025) $77.6K, +217%
Job Diversity	Job Growth (2020-2025) +24.8%	Low Unemployment (12-2025) 4.4%
Adequate Renter Ratio 52.5%	Healthy Rent Growth (5Y CAGR, 12-2025) +3.68%	Adequate Median Rent to Median Income Ratio (2025) 25.0%
Low Vacancy (2025) 9%	Low Crime Index (2025) Declining (-22%)	Highly Ranked Regionally and Nationally

Source: City-Data.com; Bestplaces.net; Apartmentlist.com; Census

CHAPTER 16

SELECTING A PROPERTY TYPE

When speaking to other investors you may often hear an alphabet soup of acronyms or codes. Herein I will demystify the terminology behind the various property classes. I will also provide some general comments on the typical business strategies operators tend to follow with each property type, so you can then form your own view on what you are comfortable with as you refine your own investment strategy and approach.

There are four classes of properties: A, B, C, and D. Each class represents a different level of risk and return.

Class A (aka Core). These properties are new (built in the last 10-15 years) or represent Class B properties that have been substantially renovated and updated. The properties are of the highest quality and boast modern construction (will often have the latest technology package and energy efficient systems). As such, these properties have the lowest amount of deferred maintenance. Class A properties have premium and several amenities (gym, dog park, office, community room, pool, spa, etc.) They are in excellent locations often close to good school districts or hip locations and high income-low crime areas. The tenant base is white collar or high income. These properties command the highest rent. Because of this, they are more sensitive to recessions and it would not be uncommon for some of the tenant base to transition to a Class B property during a recession.

Based on the above, Class A properties have a higher purchase price and as a result, lower cash on cash return and lower but more stable cash flows. They also have the greatest potential for appreciation and lowest level of risk. Cap rates tend to be the lowest as result.

Class B (aka as Core Plus). These properties were built in the last 15-30 years. Construction is generally of good quality and may be brought up to a Class B+ or Class A level after substantial renovation and modernization and thus, open an opportunity for forced appreciation via value add updates. They have some deferred maintenance and fewer amenities. They tend to be located in stable neighborhoods with moderate income and low to moderate crime areas. The tenant base is a mix of middle income professionals and higher earning blue collar workers. Rents are moderate.

Based on the above, Class B properties are less expensive than Class A properties and as a result offer moderate cash on cash return, moderate cap rate, moderate to high appreciation and moderate risk.

Class C (aka as Value Add). These properties were constructed within the last 30-60 years. The buildings have average to low functionality, are typically outdated and in need of remodel. They have much more deferred maintenance and limited (if any) amenities. Catching up to the deferred maintenance or substantial updates may bring those properties to Class C+ or B- condition, thereby creating opportunity for forced appreciation.

Class C properties are located in lower income-moderate crime areas but opportunity may be found in Class C properties located in Class B areas. Rental rates are low to moderate. The tenant base typically is comprised of blue collar/working class households. Turnover and vacancy tend to be higher.

Based on the above, Class C properties are less expensive than Class B properties and as result, offer higher cash on cash return, higher cash flow, low to moderate appreciation, and pose higher risk. Cap rates tend to be higher than those of Class A and B properties as a result thereof.

Class D (aka as Opportunistic). You may often hear those described as war zones. These are the roughest properties one can encounter. They are constructed in the last 60-100 years. They are often in poor condition and plagued with much deferred maintenance. As such, they are often obsolete with poor and outdated construction and materials and no amenities. Class D properties are located in the roughest part of town marked with violence, drugs, and prostitution. The tenant base is low income and may have a criminal record.

Based on the above, Class D properties would be the least expensive and the most risky and as a result will offer the highest cash on cash return. Cash flow may be volatile (or non-existent). Even if upgraded, based on the property location, they will rarely appreciate in value and essentially have no exit plan. They represent the highest level of risk.

Which property type you select in the end will depend on your investment parameters around acquisition costs, risk tolerance, business strategy, and desired returns.

CHAPTER 17

KEY ASSUMPTIONS TO UNDERSTAND WHEN EVALUATING A DEAL

I am sometimes asked – "I have this deal on the table. How do I know if it is a good deal?" Well, it ultimately depends on your own investment criteria and target returns as well as your comfort level with the operator. However, as you dive into the deal itself, in order to assess viability of the projections and expected returns, it is important to understand what key assumptions the operator is making when creating such projections and the business plan. Below I offer a few key assumptions to watch for and understand as you peel the onion behind the juicy returns presented to you. I dive into more detail on those and other aspects of the deal underwriting in my book Mastering Multifamily Underwriting (5 Steps to Confident, Risk-Smart Apartment Investing) available on Amazon.

1. **What are the projected rent and rent growth rate? Are they supported by rent comps and recent and future market trends?** During the 2020-2022 period, many markets experienced strong year over year rent growth (and in certain markets like Tampa or Orlando double digit

growth). This was not sustainable in the long run and sure enough, as a result of the oversupply in those and similar markets, the pace of rent growth has since adjusted down to flat levels or in some cases declined to negative rent growth (as of the time of this writing). It is important to set rent and rent growth assumptions to current market levels. While a flat 3% rent growth assumption may appear conservative on paper, if far removed from market reality, can set the investment back right off the start.

2. **What are the expenses?** Are they in line with market ($/door, % of effective gross income), the appraisal, or other public data (e.g., Costar or Yardi)? Have they been adjusted for expected taxes and insurance increases? Is the expense growth rate in line with inflation?
3. **What are the planned operating reserves? Are they adequate?** It is not uncommon to account for at least four to six months of operating expenses. If one is to be more conservative, reserving for six months of operating expense and debt service will create additional cushion and higher comfort level and reduce the risk of capital calls. Are replacement reserves in place and in line with the lender's requirements?
4. **What is the purchase price cap rate? How does it compare to market? And what is the reversion (aka exit) cap rate?** Ideally the analysis will apply the market (vs. purchase price) cap rate as the beginning point and increase that by <u>at least</u> 10 bps/year until the point of sale (a higher reversion may make sense in a low-rate environment where rates may be expected to increase). While cap rates may or may not increase by the time one sells the asset, you want to account

upfront for potential adverse fluctuations in the market. If cap rates do not increase, then you have adequate cushion.

5. **What are the finance terms (LTV, rate, tenor, interest only period, fixed or floating debt, closing costs, etc.) and are they locked in?** The lender is the largest partner in a deal. Especially in the current (as of the time of writing this book) environment where lending terms are being tightened, you want to ensure the underwriting reflects that and builds in an adequate cushion. Often the rate cannot be locked in until 7-10 days prior to closing. As such, it is important to build in a buffer in case of rate fluctuations prior to close.
6. **What is the capex budget?** Is it based on contractor bids or past experience? Are capex expenses reserved for upfront and with adequate 10% buffers (depending on the scope and nature of the project buffers range from 5% to 15%)? Especially in the current inflationary environment, it is prudent to build in some cushion.
7. **How are the waterfalls structured (do the operating agreement, private placement memorandum, and marketing presentation match)?** Are distributions a return on capital or return of capital? Is the preferred return cumulative (unpaid returns accumulate over time) or compounded (unpaid return is not only cumulative and therefore added to next year's balance but is also added to the original investment and as such, earns a preferred return on the new higher base vs. the original investment base) or neither? How are the cash flow and capital event waterfalls structured?
8. **Are there other structural considerations?** We will cover those in CHAPTER 24.

That is certainly a lot to consider. Nevertheless, these are important questions to ask so you can develop a good understanding of the underlying investment and enter into it with full awareness of the risks, cushion, and mitigating factors. I hope you now feel better equipped to dive into this next deal and evaluate the underlying assumptions behind these great returns you see in the offering memo.

And if you'd like to do a deeper dive into underwriting, along with real-life case studies, I invite you to explore **Mastering Multifamily Underwriting (5 Steps to Confident Risk-Smart Apartment Investing)**. You can find out more about it here (www.MasteringMultifamilyUnderwriting.com/book) or get your copy on Amazon.

CHAPTER 18

DEMYSTIFY THE REFINANCE IMPACT ON PASSIVE INVESTMENTS

I could see the signs of concern in her eyes when she asked worrisome: "Does it mean I will get bought out at refi?" This is a question I frequently receive from investors and pertains to the impact of refinance on one's passive investment. Below I will demystify exactly that.

Cash

In CHAPTER 13 I discuss the different waterfall structures and how the distributions flow through that. So, what happens if the sponsor determines that they want to do a **cash out refinance**?

The refinance proceeds will typically follow the capital event waterfall structure established at the onset (and documented in the private placement memorandum "PPM"). Usually, the sponsor would first pay any catch-up distributions accrued from the preferred return due but not yet paid (if the preferred return is structured as such), then they would pay down the principal investment of the LP (or a large share thereof), and lastly any excess profit would be split as per the GP-LP ownership share (for example in a 30%-70% GP-LP split, the LPs will capture 70% of such excess proceeds and the GPs the remaining 30%). Thus, ultimately the LPs will be taken care of first. Note: If the principal repayment ranks lower in the waterfall, then the profit split will precede it. Therefore, always read the PPM to see how capital event and how regular distributions will waterfall.

The LP investment principal paydown or payoff **does not dilute the ownership share**. Instead, it simply returns the principal and accumulated returns due but not yet paid back faster. The LP can then choose to reinvest such principal in other deals (or spend it however they deem appropriate).

Post payout, any preferred return would be based on the new capital account / principal balance. If such balance is zero, i.e., if the principal was fully returned to the investor at the time of refi, a pref. would not accrue and would not be paid. Instead, the waterfall will follow the established profit split (e.g., 70% LP and 30% GP in the hypothetical example above). Some deal structures will change the profit split once a certain IRR hurdle is met. Therefore, if such cash out refinance meets that IRR hurdle (typically that means the principal (or a large portion thereof) has been paid back), the profit split will change according to the new schedule established in the PPM at the onset of the deal (e.g., the split may change from 70% LP and 30% GP to 50% LP and 50% GP). This type of structure keeps the GP motivated to outperform projections and return principal back to the investors sooner.

What happens if the sponsor performs a **cash in refinance**? Unless principal is returned back to the investor, nothing will change – they will continue to receive or accrue the preferred return with profit split remaining intact. Any catch up distributions along with the gain from sale will be paid out at exit, if the deal performs as expected. A sponsor may choose to perform a cash in refinance, if they are in need of additional capital. That is a good way to source such capital utilizing the built-in equity of the deal vs. doing a cash call from investors (more on cash calls in CHAPTER 34).

Tax

There will be no tax due on the cash out or cash in refinance proceeds because the source of such proceeds is debt. In a cash out refinance scenario where principal was returned to the investors, the capital account for K1 purposes will be reduced by the distribution amount. Nevertheless, always check with your CPA re this.

CHAPTER 19

INTEREST RATE HEDGING STRATEGIES DEMYSTIFIED

I was speaking to a colleague of mine once. Unfortunately, that individual had just received the monthly financials from a syndication that they were passively invested in and was quite concerned, as the cash and cash flow were tight. In addition, the sponsor had stated that distributions were being suspended.

That particular deal, like many other deals closed in 2020-2022, was financed via a floating rate bridge loan. And while the sponsor had purchased a rate cap to partially hedge against interest rate fluctuations, such rate cap tenor was only a year (vs. the three-year loan tenor). Given the interest rate volatility, the lender had required the deal sponsor to purchase a rate cap and in the interim to start accruing for the estimated cap purchase price ahead of time (below you will understand why).

While a rate cap does help mitigate against interest rate risk volatility, there are some nuances that LPs and GPs should be aware of, so they can plan ahead and avoid unpleasant surprises (like those my friend experienced).

Below I will demystify some of the interest rate hedge strategies. This is **intended to provide a high-level overview. There are**

more technicalities within the general parameters described below and more options available that can be negotiated with a lender or a hedge provider. As such, please discuss those with your lender and cap provider (Pensford provides this service to borrowers/investors). **The below is not intended to offer advice or hedge strategies or to promote hedge products.**

I will cover the two more common interest rate hedge tools: *interest rate caps* and *interest rate swaps.*

First, there are a couple of key concepts to understand:

The **index rate or base rate**. The lender would usually charge an index rate plus a spread. The most common index rate for term loans is 30-day SOFR.

The **notional** amount = the amount that the borrower will hedge. Usually equals the principal amount of the loan.

The **tenor** = indicates when the hedge matures. Usually equals the maturity date of the loan.

The **strike** price = applicable for rate caps and collars. Usually indicates the maximum interest rate index the loan can float up or down to.

The higher the notional, the longer the tenor, and the lower the strike (especially in a rising rate or a more volatile rate environment), the higher the cap cost.

Interest Rate Cap

The interest rate cap limits how high the index rate can rise. As such, it allows the borrower to float the index interest rate up to a certain point (aka the ceiling).

The lender would typically specify the required cap tenor (usually aligned with the loan tenor, though there may be some flexibility in that requirement if the sponsor can demonstrate adequate reserves and/or DSC cushion to mitigate against interest rate volatility), the notional amount, the strike price, and the minimum required credit quality of the cap provider.

If market rates exceed the ceiling or cap rate, then the provider of the cap will make payments to the borrower sufficient enough to bring its rate back to the ceiling level. When rates are below the ceiling, no payments are made and the borrower pays market rates. The buyer of the cap/the borrower therefore enjoys a fixed rate when market rates are above the cap and a floating rate when interest rates are below the cap.

The lender may require the borrower to establish an escrow account with adequate reserves to demonstrate ability to pay the floating rate up to the rate cap index and until they receive reimbursement from the cap provider. In addition, if the cap tenor is shorter than the loan tenor, the lender would require such escrow to ensure the Borrower is able to pay the market floating rate post cap maturity or has sufficient liquidity to purchase a new rate cap until loan maturity. Cap rate costs increased exponentially during the 2022-2024 period. Per CRE Daily, in 2020, Investors Management Group was able to purchase a 5% interest rate cap for one of its properties for $22,000. In 2023, a 2-year cap would cost them $1MM!!! According to Chatham Financial and CRE Daily, "in February, the price for one-year protection on a $25MM loan with a 2% rate cap surged to $819,000 from $33,000 in early March 2022"!!!

As interest rates fall and volatility subsides, cap rate costs should fall as well but that is not an immediate adjustment.

Thus, as an LP one question you can ask the operator is whether they have established adequate reserves for that (whether or not required by the lender) and how they are mitigating the floating rates on the loan in a rising interest rate environment.

It is important to note that interest rate caps are considered options and as such, do not carry additional collateral requirements.

Exhibit 9:

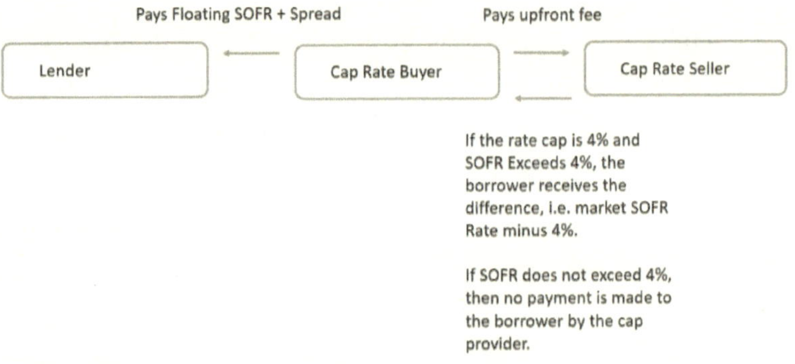

Interest Rate Swap

The interest rate swap effectively fixes the index rate at a certain level. It is mostly offered by direct lenders (smaller lenders may sometimes white label a swap provided by a larger bank). This tool swaps a floating rate with a fixed rate. If the market rate is higher than the fixed swap index rate, then the swap is in the money and the lender pays the difference to the buyer. If the market rate is lower than the fixed swap rate, then the swap is out of the money and the borrower pays for the difference in index rate to keep the swap current.

Exhibit 10:

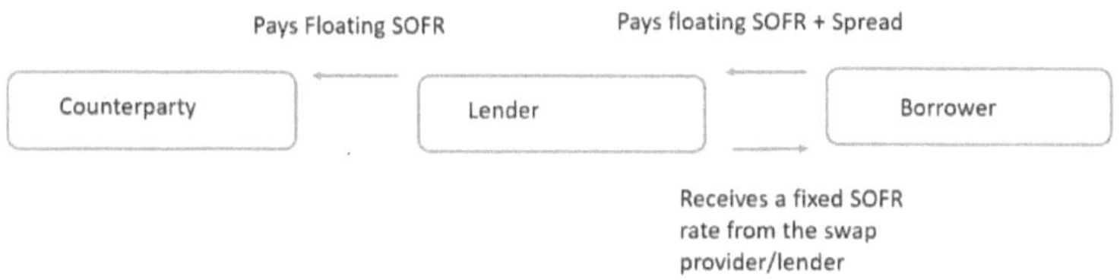

It is important to note that interest rate swaps are considered to be operating credit products and as such, typically require that the exposure is secured. If offered by the originating lender, such collateral is typically the real estate securing the loan. If offered by a third-party provider, the provider may require cash collateral or a standby letter of credit to secure the exposure.

Other interest rate hedge tools include:

Interest Rate Collars – caps how much the index rate can increase to and establishes an index floor it could fall to. Effectively the interest rate will float within that top and bottom band.

Forward Starting Swaps – may be more applicable if the borrower wants to take advantage of lower floating rate at the beginning of the term when the borrower expects that rates will increase in the future and not in the near term. Such a swap provides more flexibility than a traditional swap and therefore may cost more.

Cancellable swaps and caps – allow you the option to cancel the hedge and similar to the above, they would typically cost more for that optionality. You may even be able to sell the interest rate cap (might make sense to sell it, only if it is in the money and we are in a declining interest rate environment). The interest rate cap option value decreases the closer the cap gets to its expiry date.

CHAPTER 20

THE PASSIVE INVESTOR'S GUIDE TO INVESTMENT OFFERING WEBINARS AND THE PERFECT PRESENTATION DECK

The time has arrived! You have found a sponsor that you know, like, and trust! You have done your research and gotten educated on the market(s) of your interest and how to vet investment opportunities. Now awaiting in your inbox is an invitation to join an informational webinar on a new investment your sponsor has carefully curated. What is next?

You may feel nervous about what to expect, especially if this is your first investment. Not to worry! Below I will demystify the typical webinar structure and what to expect so you can be well prepared.

In addition, as you dive deeper and deeper into syndications and alternative investments like real estate, you will likely encounter a variety of investment offering presentations. They come in all shapes and sizes. Therefore, I thought I'd take a moment to also share the key sections you should look for in an investment offering presentations. If you see any of those missing, it should at least prompt a question (or two or more ☺) to your lead sponsor to provide you with the clarity and needed transparency on those.

First, ensure you register for the webinar, so you can receive the recording as unexpected or last-minute scheduling conflicts may arise.

Logistical set up

The sponsor team would typically open with covering logistical matters such as reminder of the forthcoming recording and when to expect it, mute/unmute etiquette, how and when to ask questions, and outline of the call.

Intro of the team

They will then proceed with introduction of the company and the management team and will briefly speak to their background, experience, and the collective track record. This is particularly helpful if you are not familiar with the other team members. At the end of the day, the sponsor can make or break a deal – getting clarity on the captains and co-captains and what specific role(s) they play is key. A typical sponsorship team would not have more than 5 key members. You want to see at least 3 (for succession and key man risk mitigation purposes). Seeing too many managers (GPs) raises the question on what their unique role is, especially if the deal is not large enough.

The operator/ lead sponsor's track record. Most presentations will lead with that section and share who the lead operator/fund manager team is. Ideally such track record will speak not only to the team's overall portfolio size and geographic footprint, but will also share details on how such existing deals are performing (relative to the original underwrite projections) and how their exits performed (e.g., purchase and sale price, overall returns, and actual vs projected returns and NOI). For operators with sizeable portfolios, this information may be made available via a data room (vs. squeezing it in 5pt size font on a single slide or two).

The market. This is key, as after all the market can be the tail wind behind a deal. The market will also drive the underlying underwrite assumptions and will paint the story on why the business plan makes sense. This is why understanding the larger market and the local sub-market is key.

The business plan. As investors we get paid to take risk and we need to be appropriately compensated for the risk. Being able to force appreciation when acquiring an asset (ideally on a good basis) is key in optimizing profits and achieving target returns. This is why it is important to understand the business plan, how the operator intends to add value, why that plan makes sense (relative to the current market conditions and relative to their prior track record executing on similar investments). This is also where the sponsor will share an overview of the property (which overview will showcase key amenities, if any, and photos).

The underwrite. The fun part of the presentation (at least for me) is usually the financial overview where the sponsor will walk through the sources and uses of funds, how capex will be utilized, debt terms, projected performance over the intended hold period, and proforma returns.

In most cases, the presentation will likely not have a slide showing the full underwriting spreadsheet as it can be quite detailed and with multiple tabs. However, they should at least have a snippet of the baseline T12 (trailing 12 month) financials and the 5-year pro forma (if the intended hold period is 5 years) showing the numbers all the way down to the cash flow after debt service and fees level. This is where the pro forma assumptions should align with the market, business plan, and finance structure.

Naturally it may be difficult to follow that many numbers on a screen. Thus, should you feel you want to dig deeper, you can always reach out to the sponsor after the call and request a copy of their model and underwrite (ideally in an unlocked Excel format).

Sensitivity analysis. A comprehensive presentation will also include the sensitivity analysis that shows the various return outcomes should one or more underlying assumptions vary. After all, projections are just that – projections. The pro forma numbers are not set in stone and remain subject to the market and the operator's ability to execute. As such, it is important to understand what the return profile looks like if key variables, like rent growth or cap rates, do not come out as expected.

Comp analysis (rent and sales). Some presentations will include comp analysis in their Appendix. As this information is typically an eye chart, the operator might make it available via a data room instead.

Key risks and mitigates. Very few offering presentations include this slide but it is an important one. While the private placement memorandum will typically outline any and all risks associated with a particular investment, it is important to understand the three to five key risks of a deal as well as how they are mitigated and whether you think the mitigates outlined by the presenter are reasonable (this is where understanding the market, the underwrite, the business plan, and the operator's track record comes in handy). This particular section will outline what can realistically go wrong and what action plan the sponsor has today to minimize the adverse impact of such event(s).

Next Steps

Before they open the forum for questions, each presentation should conclude with clear next steps on how to invest and key contact information of the person you can connect with to obtain additional information or raise follow up questions.

Such next steps may include – how to submit a soft commit, a link to the investment portal, funding deadlines, types of funds accepted (e.g., if investing via a self-directed IRA or via a 1031 exchange is an option), min and max investment amount, etc.

Appendix

If included, this section will usually share the rent comps, sales comps, and any other information pertinent to the investment.

Not all investment decks are made equal. However, a strong presentation will have the key components above.

Q&A

In the end, the sponsor will open it up to questions. Usually, they will start with pre-submitted questions to kick things off, followed by questions in the chat, and lastly live questions. Especially if this is your first webinar, you can learn a ton from the questions of others and apply those learnings as you evaluate future investment opportunities.

Follow up one on one with the sponsor post the webinar

You likely have the sponsor's contact information by now, given your pre-existing relationship. Thus, should you prefer to ask questions one on one or if you have follow-up queries, you can always reach out to him/her directly. They will be more than happy to address all your follow up questions and comments to ensure you make an informed investment decision.

You can expect a copy of the presentation, a link to the recording, and link to the investment portal after the call.

Should there be multiple follow up queries, it would not be unusual for the sponsor to set up a Follow Up Q&A call, dedicated solely to addressing follow up queries. This is where many investors will dig deeper into the details or seek further clarification, i.e., attending those calls can be not only informative for the particular deal but also educational (in terms of what other investors are looking for when making investment decisions, how they ask the questions, how the sponsor handles those).

The more investment offering webinars you attend and the more investment offering presentations you see, the more familiar and comfortable you will be with the structure and participation live. Attending those calls will also help you get to know various sponsors better – you will start seeing the difference in investment philosophy and approach across various groups and sponsors and deals. And over time before you know it you will be one of the experienced investors taking part in those calls!

PART 4

HOW TO VET OPERATORS (#1 RISK IN SYNDICATIONS)

CHAPTER 21

HOW TO PROPERLY VET A REAL ESTATE SPONSOR BEFORE YOU INVEST

One of the most important lessons I learned during my years as a commercial lender reviewing hundreds of real estate transactions is this:

The deal rarely fails because of the spreadsheet. It fails because of the people behind it.

Spreadsheets can be adjusted. Assumptions can be optimized. Markets can shift.

But the operator - their discipline, judgment, integrity, and ability to navigate challenges - is what ultimately determines whether a deal succeeds or struggles.

This is why you will often hear the phrase:

"Bet on the jockey, not the horse."

In this chapter, I will walk you through a structured, step-by-step approach to properly vet a sponsor or operator. The goal is not to find a "perfect" track record. That does not exist. The goal is to develop the ability to **identify capable, disciplined, and aligned operators - and avoid those who are not.**

Step 1 - Start with the Human Element: Know Who You Are Investing With

Before analyzing track record, returns, or business plans, start with something more fundamental:

Who is this person, and how do they operate?

Real estate, despite the data and analytics, remains a **relationship-driven business**. You are entering into what is often a multi-year partnership. Understanding the individual behind the deal is critical.

What to Look For:

- Have they made an effort to understand your investment goals?
- Do they educate, or do they only sell?
- How do they communicate outside of active deals (newsletters, insights, updates)?
- Are they consistent in their messaging and approach?

Why This Matters

Over time, patterns emerge. You begin to see how they think, how they communicate, how they treat investors, and whether they are long-term relationship builders or transactional.

This stage is less about asking perfect questions and more about **observing behavior over time**.

Practical Actions

- Attend their webinars or presentations
- Read their newsletters and thought leadership
- Schedule introductory calls without an immediate deal in front of you
- Interact with them in low-pressure settings

You are not just evaluating competence. You are evaluating **character and consistency**.

Step 2 - Evaluate Experience and Track Record (With Context, Not Just Headlines)

Experience matters. But more importantly, **relevant experience and how that experience was earned** matter. Past performance is not always a predictor of future performance; however, it is a helpful indicator.

What to Assess:

1. Investment approach

More specifically, understand their risk appetite, what markets and sub-markets they focus on, how they create value (value add vs. turnkey), investment strategy (cash flow or appreciation) and what asset class they focus on. Then determine how that compares to your personal investing strategy and criteria.

For example, if you are a cash flow investor, like me, then a sponsor focusing on new development (which carries higher risk and the payout is delayed until the time of sale) might not be a good fit for you. If you are more conservative, then the stable value-add strategy (which has cushion against market fluctuations vs. buying a turnkey asset and relying on appreciation) may be a better fit for you.

2. Depth of Experience

- How long have they been investing or operating?
- How many deals have they completed?
- How many have gone full cycle?

Time in the market mitigates operational risk, as over time the operators build knowledge and experience that can help them structure deals more conservatively, plan better, or be able to pivot more efficiently during a period of challenge.

3. Relevance of Experience

- Do they specialize in the asset class you are investing in or are they all over the place in terms of markets and asset classes?
- Have they operated similar deal types (e.g., value-add vs. development, 20 unit vs. 200-unit properties, Class C vs. Class A properties, etc.)?
- Do they have experience in that specific market?
- If their real estate experience is limited, what is their business experience? Have they successfully run and operated a business? Have they performed well and been in a leadership position?

4. Experience Through Cycles

- Have they operated through both strong and challenging markets?
- Or is their track record concentrated in a favorable cycle (e.g., 2011–2021)?

The Most Important Question to Ask: How did actual NOI performance compare to projections?

This is where many investors stop short. A deal that performed well during a period of cap rate compression may not reflect true operational strength. I'd still give the operator credit for making a decision to exit when cap rates are low (i.e., top of the market) vs. getting caught up in the market hype or in hopes and dreams (aka greed) of better returns. However, what matters is:

- Did they achieve projected NOI?
- Were rent growth assumptions realistic?
- Did they control expenses effectively?

What you are really trying to determine is whether success has been driven by operational execution consistently or by market tailwinds and timing. The distinction is critical.

Step 3 - Understand the Team, Not Just the Individual

Multifamily and commercial real estate are **team sports**. Even highly capable individuals rely on a broader team to execute the business plan.

Therefore, understanding the overall sponsorship team, their roles and responsibilities, key person risk, and the overall team/company structure is important. Ideally there will be at least two or three and no more than five-six key people on the management team. Thus, if something was to happen to one, there are others to see through the business plan and serve as a point of contact.

Key Areas to Evaluate

1. Team Structure

- Who are the key decision-makers?
- What are their roles and responsibilities?
- Is there clarity in who handles acquisitions, asset management, capital raising, and operations?

2. Depth, Redundancy, and Key Person Risk

- Is there a bench, or does everything depend on one person?
- What happens if a key individual is no longer involved?

You should always ask: **What happens if the lead sponsor is no longer able to operate the business?**

Look for a capable supporting team, defined processes and systems, and key man insurance, if applicable. The goal is to ensure the business plan is not dependent on a single individual.

3. History of Working Together

- Is this a long-standing team?
- Or a newly assembled group for this specific deal?

Ad hoc teams can work. However, they introduce additional risk if relationships, communication styles, and decision-making processes are untested.

Step 4 - Evaluate Alignment of Interests and Risk Discipline

Alignment is one of the most important, yet often misunderstood, aspects of sponsor evaluation. To vet that there are a couple of areas to explore.

Skin in the Game

Ask:

- Is the sponsor investing their own capital in the deal?
- How meaningful is that investment relative to their net worth?
- How much is the GP team collectively putting in?

It is not uncommon for the sponsorship team to put in between 5% and 10% equity in the deal. Ideally this would be fresh equity vs. rolling in the full or partial acquisition fee raised into the deal. Without stating the obvious, meaningful co-investment signals confidence, accountability, and alignment with investors.

Beyond Equity - True Alignment

Equity alone is not enough. You also want to understand:

- Are they providing a loan guarantee, especially if they are not contributing meaningful equity in the deal?

- Are they financially exposed beyond fees?
- Is the fee structure aligned with prioritizing performance and LPs?

True alignment means the sponsor **wins when investors win and feels the downside when investors feel it.**

Risk Awareness and Transparency

One of the most telling questions you can ask is: **"Why should I NOT do this deal?"** This question will naturally lead to a discussion of key risks and how/to what extent they are mitigated. Unexpected things always happen. Thus, you want to see if the sponsor has thought through the potential risks and everything that can go wrong as well as what actions they are taking today to minimize the adverse impact and how they are planning for unexpected events.

A strong operator will clearly articulate risks, explain how they are mitigating them, and avoid overly optimistic or dismissive answers.

Be cautious of sponsors who minimize risks, rely heavily on best-case scenarios, and cannot clearly explain downside protections.

Step 5 - Analyze How the Sponsor Performs When Things Go Wrong

Every experienced operator has had deals that did not go as planned. If they say they have not, that is a red flag. Especially if the operator has been in business long enough, they will have at least one deal that did not go as planned or potentially lost money. I am yet to meet investors who have 100% batting average. Looking for the perfect track record is not the point. However, it is important to understand what they learned from these challenges (losses), how such experiences helped them become savvier investors over time, and why they are confident they can avoid making the same mistake in the future.

Questions to Ask

- Can you share an example of a deal that underperformed?
- What went wrong?
- What did you do to address it?
- What did you learn?

What You Are Looking For

- accountability (no blame shifting)
- transparency
- decisive action
- lessons learned and applied

This is often where you gain the **deepest insight into the operator's true capabilities**.

Capital Calls and Paused Distribution History

You should always ask:

- Have they ever issued a capital call?
- Have they ever paused distributions?

More importantly: **Why?**

Not all capital calls are bad. And unexpected things happen. However, the cause matters:

- unforeseen external events
- conservative vs. aggressive underwriting
- reserve planning
- execution quality

Most importantly, one should understand what they learned from the experience and how they are applying such learning in their business and processes today. What you are evaluating is **decision-making and learning**, not perfection.

Step 6 - Evaluate Communication and Transparency

Strong communication is not a "nice to have." It is a core component of a successful investor relationship.

What to Evaluate

1. Frequency and Quality of Reporting

- How often do they provide updates?
- Are reports clear, detailed, and easy to understand?

You can always request a copy of past communications and reporting.

2. Accessibility

- Are they available for questions?
- Do they respond in a timely, transparent, and thoughtful manner?

3. Tax and Financial Reporting

- Do they deliver K-1s on time?
- Are financials organized, clear, and consistent?

4. The Most Important Aspect of Communication: How do they communicate bad news?

Anyone can deliver good news. Pay close attention to tone, clarity, level of detail, and willingness to take responsibility.

Ask for examples of past communications during challenging situations. This will tell you far more than polished investor presentations.

After you have had an opportunity to ask these questions and assess the data, ask yourself how your gut feels. That is just as important as you enter into this (hopefully long-term) relationship.

Step 7 - Conduct Independent Verification

Do not rely solely on sponsor-provided information. Verify before you trust by:

- Performing detailed background checks. A well-done background check can uncover important information that may not be otherwise publicly available. I often like to be upfront about performing one and give the operator the benefit of sharing anything of relevance and importance upfront. If you find something of concern that they have been upfront about, then at least you know they are not hiding and open to having a deeper follow up conversation about it to address any outstanding questions or concerns. And if they do not share, that is an easy red flag to put pencils down and move on.

- Requesting references from current and past investors
- Speaking with investors who did not reinvest and ask why. Sometimes there could be timing or personal circumstances for their decision. However, if they had a poor experience, they will talk about it.
- Searching public records and litigation history
- Leveraging investor communities and forums for additional feedback re prior experience with that sponsor

A strong operator should be comfortable with this level of diligence.

Transparency builds trust. Resistance raises questions.

Final Thought - Trust Your Process, Not Just Your Instincts

There are always risks with investing but proper diligence upfront can help mitigate those and set you on a path of success as you continue your investing journey.

After completing your diligence, you may still ask: **"How do I know if this is the right sponsor?"**

There is no perfect answer. However, a structured process helps you move beyond intuition alone and evaluate: character, experience, alignment, discipline, and communication.

Your instincts still matter. But they should be informed by data, observation, and thoughtful analysis.

At the end of the day, you are not just investing in a deal. You are partnering with a team for multiple years, through both favorable and challenging environments.

Choose that partner carefully.

Top Strategies to Find an Operator That You Know, Like, and Trust

Earlier we discussed top questions to ask the deal sponsor(s) and how to do diligence on the sponsor. However, a question that often comes up is - how do you even find sponsors you want to invest with? Below I'll offer a few ideas.

1. **Local real estate meet ups.** Meet Ups are a great venue where you can meet operators that reside in your area. Often such operators are speakers at such local events, which allows you an opportunity to meet them in person one on one after the meeting and get to know them.
2. **Conferences.** Another great opportunity to connect with sponsors in person are conferences. These may happen to be outside of your local area. However, they

would allow you an opportunity to meet a wider array of sponsors who you might not otherwise have connected with or perhaps sponsor you saw on social media and want to complete the connection with via an in-person interaction.

3. **Real Estate Podcasts.** Podcasts are a good way to learn about various sponsors, their investment philosophy, investments strategy, and even hear about past deals they worked on and how those turned out or seminars they faced and what they learned from those. Podcast hosts would often ask personal questions too, which would allow you to get to know them on a personal level.
4. **Referrals from other LPs.** Referrals are a great way to find sponsors as the investors sharing those names with you have presumably already had a positive investing experience with them and can provide their personal and non-marketing perspective. Conversely, fellow investors may also share negative experiences, which would provide insights into which sponsors to avoid.
5. **Social Media-Newsletters.** Many sponsors today are on social media (Facebook, Instagram, LinkedIn, YouTube, etc.) and have their own web sites, which allows you to passively follow them or interact with them online and get to know them over time. Most sponsors issue periodic newsletters as well, in an effort to stay connected with their investment community. Subscribing to such newsletters will give you an insight into their communication style, the types of deals they are working on, and how they think and operate.

6. **Investment Clubs and Forums.** Investment clubs are groups of investors that get together to evaluate deals and potentially pool their collective money to invest in deals. Group members will often exchange ideas and share experiences, which would be a great resource for sponsor referrals (and even sponsors to avoid). There are several groups out there that one can look into.

Once you identify sponsors that you like, what's next? Get to know them over time and ideally meet them in person or at least over Zoom. This would allow both parties to develop a relationship over time. At the end of the day, despite the prevalence of social media and technology, real estate remains a belly-to-belly business where in-person interaction is essential in building strong relationships and also a great tool to vet your potential partners.

Evaluating An Operator/Lead Sponsor's Risk Management Practices

"Risk management is a more realistic term than safety. It implies that hazards are ever-present, that they must be identified, analyzed, evaluated, and controlled or rationally accepted."

—Felix Beck

Those of you who have been following me for a while have likely heard me talk about taking calculated risk. While investing in real estate, and multifamily in particular, has many benefits, it does not come without a risk. The one guarantee I will make is that risk is always present. Just like with any investment, there is a real risk of loss of capital. This reminds me of my own experience as a former commercial lender when I had to take calculated risk when lending multi-millions to borrowers in the middle market space.

While one cannot eliminate risk, one can think through the possible risks upfront and ways to mitigate them for an optimal outcome.

Below I'll cover a few of the key risks common to multifamily investing and offer a few mitigation strategies for passive investors to be aware of, so they can be better positioned to evaluate deals and the deal sponsor's risk management.

1. **Cash Flow Risk.** A lower-than-expected rental income or higher than expected expenses could quickly lead to thinner or potentially negative NOI. Having optimistic or aggressive assumptions not supported by current data, can quickly lead a deal from hero to zero.
    - This is why, as a way to risk mitigate potential variability, it is important to have realistic assumptions about projected rent growth, vacancy (physical and economic), and expenses (adjusted for tax and insurance), validated by third parties like the lender, property manager, insurance broker, boots on the ground contact. You can reference our step-by-step key assumptions blueprint on this topic in CHAPTER 17.

2. **Valuation Risk.** If anyone knew where markets would be, that person would likely be betting or consulting hedge funds. As such, it is not only important to buy the deal right (see the APPENDIX on how to quickly and efficiently vet a deal for success), but also to prudently think through the exit valuation. If markets rise, then there is only an upside. However, if markets contract (leading to cap rate reversion), that can have material impact on valuations.
    - Projecting cap rate expansion throughout the tenor of the hold period is one way to manage the risk of potential market fluctuations.
3. **Market Risk.** In CHAPTER 15 I discuss the importance of knowing the market and submarket and questions one should ask for preliminary diligence. In addition, understanding the demand and supply dynamics and absorption trends is key. In 2023-2024, many submarkets (with otherwise strong KPIs) were impacted by new supply of multifamily entering the market in an environment where household formation was slowing down, resulting in rent decline and increased vacancy.
    - Making sure the property has adequate cushion as measured by low break-even occupancy and adequate operating reserves is one way to mitigate the risk upfront. In addition, having multiple exit strategies provides optionality and additional flexibility to pivot if/as needed.
4. **Economics Risk.** If a recession is to occur, are the employers in the area recession resistant or diversified

enough? Does the property have particular tenant concentration? Is this a one-employer town? Do tenants have adequate household income? All of these factors can impact the property performance.

- Selecting markets that have multiple employers, preferably export related and recession resistant, diversified employer base, and minimum median household income of $50K helps mitigate such economic risk (over time this minimum should adjust with inflation).

5. **Interest Rate Risk.** Macroeconomic, global, and geopolitical factors can impact interest rate movements. And as we saw in the 2022-2023 period, those can quickly change over a short period of time.

   - I am not in the game of speculating where rates would be. As such, I like to lock in fixed rate debt. Not all debt providers have that option but they would be able to offer risk mitigation tools such as swaps or caps to mitigate the interest rate fluctuation risk (discussed in CHAPTER 19).

6. **Operational Risk.** This pertains to the operator's/key sponsor's ability to run the property, which includes managing the property manager, lease up, marketing, maintenance, managing the rehab (if applicable).

   - Understanding the operator's performance track record, how they handled prior mistakes or challenges, their business and real estate background is key. In addition, I prefer to work with vertically-integrated operators, as that keeps them one step closer to the asset and operations. Alternatively, if a third-party property manager is hired, I want to understand their track record and how long they've worked with that sponsor.

7. **Legal Risk.** As the name suggests, this pertains to the risk of lawsuits or other legal matters like zoning, title, building code compliance, licenses required to operate the property
   - There are a number of ways to mitigate this potential risk, including working with a licensed real estate and SEC attorney at the onset of setting up the investment opportunity. In addition, working with a property manager and being well versed in the local and regional regulatory requirements is imperative. Last but not least, having adequate insurance that not only provides liability mitigation but also loss of risk coverage, including lost rental income in a natural disaster scenario.
8. **Liquidity Risk.** There is nothing worse than running out of money at the onset or in the middle of a deal. A lot of unexpected events could happen.
   - How one can help mitigate against such risk is having adequate operating reserves (ideally at least six months of operating expenses AND debt service) and capex reserves with contingency cushion (at least 10% or more) from the beginning.
9. **Refinance And Finance Risk.** Those working on live deals in mid-2022 to early 2023 likely remember many situations where the lender walked away or changed material terms to the deal in the last minute. Certainty

of close is important, especially when working through so many variables during the diligence.

- While one cannot control the lending landscape, working with a broker or a lender with a proven track record of closing deals usually helps. They may not be the least expensive ones but you get what you pay for.

  In addition, when evaluating investment opportunities, I do not bake in a refinance in the numbers. A refinance, which in most cases (2022-2023 were an exception) returns the initial principal investment in full or in part, typically inflates projected returns. I do not want to depend on a refinance to meet projected returns, especially if the rate environment happens to be unfavorable to refinance at that future point of time.

I recognize we covered a lot but hope the above provides a streamlined blueprint on the key risks to consider. I'd like to end on a positive note from Benjamin Graham I often refer to:

> "*The essence of investment management is the management of risks, not the management of returns.*"
>
> —Benjamin Graham

CHAPTER 22

TOP STRATEGIES TO AVOID INVESTMENT SCAMS

A Framework, A Personal Lesson, and What Recent Cases Reveal

In the preceding chapter, we discussed how to evaluate a legitimate operator's capabilities and alignment. In this chapter, we shift to a different and more serious risk - how to identify situations where the investment itself may not be what it appears.

A Practical Framework to Spot Red Flags

"SEC Halts $155 Million Fraudulent
Oil and Gas Offering Scheme"

"A real estate guru peddling the 'deal of a lifetime'
was really a fraud, prosecutors say"

"SEC Charges Convicted Fraudster in
Real Estate Ponzi Scheme"

These are just a few of the headlines that made their way across my desk between 2022 and 2024. With the distress in the market resulting in tighter cash flow and capital calls (and in some cases losses such as the large Houston apartment portfolio foreclosure that was all over the press), passive investors are more likely to raise concerns and complain to the Securities and Exchange Commission (SEC). As a result, such headlines are likely to be even more frequent.

According to the Federal Trade Commission, investment fraud is among the top five categories of fraud, with losses nearly doubling from $1.8 billion to $3.8 billion. The continued development of Artificial Intelligence will likely make fraud even more difficult to detect.

In my career I have been able to stop three fraudulent schemes. Based on my own experience, the signs of fraud are not always financial.

Rather than focus on why these events occur, I want to focus on what we can learn from them.

Below is a practical framework you can use to better assess investment opportunities and identify potential red flags.

1. **Real people.** Meet the sponsor and the operator. Ultimately you want to ensure you are doing real business with real people. Are they public figures and well known in their community and the industry? How long have they been in business? What is their overall reputation among other active investors, passive investors, and strategic partners such as attorneys, insurance brokers, lenders?
2. **Real business.** Visit the asset or have someone you trust do a drive by or walk the premises, if you are not local to

the area. Sponsors may not always offer to have LPs tour the property during diligence due to seller constraints. However, you will at least have the address (to do a visit) and can then review the purchase and sale agreement or other offering documents to confirm the subject asset is the one listed in the documents, including title reports. Syndication investment are regulated by the SEC and documents and investment offerings are handled by licensed SEC attorneys, which serves as another checkpoint on this.

3. **History of operations.** How long the particular sponsors have or the group he/she is partnering with been in business? What is their track record (we discussed in detail in CHAPTER 21)?
4. **Guaranteed or high returns over a short period of time.** If something is too good to be true, it is probably not true or at a minimum comes with a higher level of risk. Real estate is a long-term play. Especially in multifamily value add projects, it takes some time to stabilize the property (at least a year as most leases have 12-month terms). Some capex projects even take longer as realistically speaking, not all projects are completed at the same time for example. No one can predict where the markets will be either. For example, no one could have foreseen that the Fed would raise rates 12 times in 15-18 months. All that to say that, that one should at least try to understand the drivers for such projections and for guarantees of immediate and high returns.
5. **Understand the underlying business model (especially for alternative investments where you are**

underwriting the operating business too vs. plain vanilla apartments). If you cannot clearly explain how the business generates cash flow, that is a risk in itself. Complexity often hides risk.

I was presented with a similar investment opportunity as the one in the article noted above (though the one I reviewed was in oil and gas). The risk profile and cash flow stream timing did not align with my own investment criteria, and so I passed. However, beyond that I also felt that I did not have sufficient understanding of the business model. As it was outside of my investment parameters and I had decided to pass, I did not peel the onion further. Unfortunately, as noted in the article, the operators kept raising money both directly with investors and via other sponsors who may or may not have taken the time to peel the onion.

6. **Perform background checks on the sponsor team.** While doing that will not prevent future misdeeds, it at least provides a look back history. For example, if anyone had looked up Bernie Madoff, they would likely not have found derogatory criminal history. In fact, he passed three SEC audits before his Ponzi scheme was uncovered (it was uncovered during the market downturn, see a commonality here?). In the SEC fraudster article above, the sponsor was previously indicted in 2008 and had been just released out of jail in 2017. However, he operated under an alias and a different company name (see points #1-3 above).
7. **Lack of transparency or transactions that are too complex to understand.** The real estate guru article or

my personal story of the oil and gas carbon recapture (see #5 above) are good example of that. The sponsor should be able to explain to you in simple terms how cash flow will be generated and what the associated risk is. If they are not sharing the requested information or if they become defensive or appear frustrated (or even agitated when you continue to press for the answer or to ask additional questions), these are red flags you may want to pay attention to.

8. **Ponzi schemes where new investors feed current investors** - e.g., Madoff or the two SEC articles above, which unfortunately are one of many examples. Such Ponzi schemes tend to do well in up markets and quickly crumble during a shock or a market downturn.
9. **High pressure to move quickly and rush through the information skipping over details or leaving questions unanswered.** While it is true that once a property is under contract, there is a limited amount of time to close and while in addition SEC regulations dictate when investment opportunities can be first shared with investors (which further compresses the timeline), there is usually a period of about thirty days give or take (depending on the deal) where investors have an opportunity to review the materials, ask questions, etc. If you feel too rushed to move (and without being provided with the information needed to make an investment decision), then you might want to wait for the next opportunity.
10. **Third Party validation by other parties** like CPAs, attorneys, lenders, insurance companies. Now, this is

NOT always a guarantee of a clean slate (Ask me how I know!). However, it at least brings some comfort that various other (licensed) professionals have vetted the deal and/or the sponsor/sponsor group over a period of time.

Even with all these checkpoints unfortunately, one may still fall victim of fraud, especially when dealing with sophisticated criminals. Nevertheless, ask the questions you feel and think you need to ask. Peel the onion. Look under the hood, if you can. And most importantly, trust your gut.

Frameworks are helpful. But they only become real when tested in the field. And sometimes, even when you believe you have done everything right, things still go wrong.

Lessons Learned from A Now Troubled Investment I Passively Invested In

It was a beautiful day in May. The sun was shining, birds were chirping. Life was good. I was getting ready to head out to an investor meet up when the email came in…notifying me that my distribution was going to be delayed by three months and converted from monthly to quarterly.

The explanation included a list of personal circumstances, followed by what I can only describe as excuses. None of them justified a sudden pause in distributions (e.g., business seasonality - not something new, regulatory and compliance requirements - which do not typically pop up overnight, certain transaction types falling through - which transactions were not supposed to be part of the fund structure to begin with, etc.).

My blood froze. Various emotions started going through my mind and heart. Being a full-time investor, I depended on this passive income...

What followed was an initial request for information I sent to the syndicator I had invested through, followed by numerous follow ups, which yielded no results. No information was shared with me (and I was told none had been shared with other LPs or other syndicators raising capital for that operator).

Given the operator had gone dark, I could only think the worst – both my principal investment and income stream were gone.

Unfortunately, as limited partners (LPs) we do not have control over the daily decisions. And absent fraud, the agreement had very onerous provisions re suing the operator.

The one thing I could walk away with are the lessons learned, which I thought I would share with you today and hopefully save you from entering into a similar situation and help you avoid pain.

I had done all the diligence, or so I thought, including but not limited to: understanding the business model, discussing the investment and operator with other passive investors who invested either via the syndicator I invested through or directly with the operator, checking the track record and full cycles box, understanding what type of diligence the syndicator had done on the operator, reading through the offering documents, etc.

Yet looking back and knowing what I know now, there are a few lessons this experience taught me and things I could have done better (in other words would do differently going forward).

(By way of background, this investment was NOT in multifamily. I had chosen it as a way to introduce some diversification to my own portfolio while at the same time adhering to my primary investment objective – cash flow).

Trust But Verify

Just because someone is well known or recognized on social media or been in the business for a long time does not mean they would be transparent in communicating or running a strong operation. The 10+ year period this operator had been in business coincided with the post 2009-2011 boom, i.e., a period when everyone did well, capital was abundant, and business was good.

Just because they are large or have been in business for a long time does not mean they have internal operations and books and records in order.

Part of my frustration when I received the bad news was that no financial information was shared – historical or projected.

What I could have done differently:

- Request a copy of the historical financials of the company (both for the fund and for the underlying business).
- Review a sample of the monthly/quarterly reporting (which I subsequently found out was none).
- Validate the diligence the syndicator I invested through had done on the operator. While I understood what it was, I could have requested a copy of their reports and data or even a copy of the periodic reporting they are receiving from the operators (which unfortunately

turned out to be none and the syndicator had not bothered to ask).

Read The PPM More Diligently to Detect LP Hostile Terms

The agreement allowed for material changes without notice (such as changing the distribution schedule or pausing distributions).

In addition, any disputes could only be resolved in a specific state (designated by the operator) and no class action lawsuits were allowed, with fees to be covered by the plaintiff (irrespective of which party dominates).

While the operator may or may not be willing to update such clauses and sections, at a minimum having a discussion upfront about it to understand what, if any, options are available is key. How they respond to the question and what other offsetting LP friendly terms they have would also play a factor in my comfort level as I assess whether to proceed or not.

Diversify, Diversify, Diversify

Part of the reason I had chosen the investment and the operator was the stability of cash flow and ability to diversify my own portfolio (as an active investor I focus on stable value add apartments in the South East). However, over time I had increased my position with that syndicator to a point where a material portion of my passive income was being generated from this investment/syndicator. What started as diversification became concentration. Even though things started off well and were going well, I probably should have diversified to other investments to minimize the risk of being dependent on this income stream.

Avoid Promotional Offers and Trust Your Gut

The last two funds I invested in had promotional offers (one was offering a higher dividend and the other offered to start distributions sooner than usual). Now I know there was a reason for that. Also at the time, particularly with the last fund, I recall having that gut feeling and being really torn. The funding deadline was fast approaching. Unfortunately, I made the decision to move forward and increase my position. Knowing what I know now, I would have quieted that fear of missing out and the yearning for a (what at the time I perceived and expected to be) steady income stream.

What troubled me most about the situation was the lack of communication and transparency. I am not sure how you control for that (especially since all third party and LP feedback I had received up to that point had been positive…likely because the operator had not gone through a rough patch).

As I conclude writing this summary of lessons learned, I still feel pain and quite vulnerable. But I thought it is more important to put my feelings aside and share the key takeaways with you in an effort to save you from experiencing a similar situation as a passive investor.

If my experience was an isolated case, it would be easier to dismiss. Unfortunately, it is not. The recent rise in Ponzi schemes and fraudulent offerings reveals broader patterns that every investor should understand.

My Thoughts on Recent Ponzi Schemes

Former CEO of Orange County-Based Private Equity Fund Charged with Conning Investors Out of $62.5 Million via Bogus Promissory Notes

Florida woman who led a nearly $200 million Ponzi scheme sentenced to 20 years in prison

Alex Mehr and Tai Lopez accused of running $112 million Ponzi scheme

It feels like these Ponzi schemes have been popping up like mushrooms after rain. I have been coming across more of those lately. I thought I'd provide my thoughts on the topic not to add to the negative news you may be reading lately but rather to share a few key takeaways that directly apply to investing in real estate too.

Unfortunately, there is no easy way to tell fraud is present as the signs are not always obvious. I previously shared a few key strategies to spot a scam as well as my own learnings from a failed investment (which was officially declared as a Ponzi scheme eventually too). However, this recent news triggers a few additional observations that I want to share for your consideration.

In most cases the dominos fall during periods of market contractions and down cycles.

What this means is that we, as investors, should be on high alert during good times (or at least be prudent enough to exit during good times), if we are invested in a deal that is too good to be true. It is not uncommon for Ponzi schemes to trigger claw back provisions, however. Thus, any earnings above and beyond recovery of the principal investment could be clawed back by the authorities because those profits were effectively generated with new investors' money.

Understand the underlying business structure and cash/cash flow paper trail.

How does the business make money? How is it capitalized? Are these real people with real assets and real business?

In the Florida woman example case, where the core business activity was providing short-term merchant cash advances, you would want to understand the operator's vetting process and credit policies when extending credit, who their customers are (consumers or businesses), their bad debt and allowance for losses and how that compares to actual, their loan loss ratio, the collection and portfolio management processes, the repayment rate, the underlying client contracts, etc. That is not to say contracts cannot be falsified but if you request sufficient information along with financials (see below), discrepancies may pop up.

In the Marco Santarelli's case, investors were promised returns generated from a variety of businesses including e-commerce, real estate, Broadway shows, and cryptocurrency (i.e., lack of focus and expertise on a single area of business). Assuming one jumped into the hodge podge portfolio, it would be important to understand how each of these underlying asset classes generates cash flow, request copies of their financials and the bank statements showing the incoming deposits, understand the operator's background and experience in these areas.

In the case of Tai Lopez, the business plan was quite logical - buy distressed companies with physical retail locations, leverage his/his partners ecommerce expertise to boost online sales, turn them around, and exit at a healthy multiple. All investor calls were touting continuous revenue but there was no detailed discussion on profits. While financials were provided, they turned out to be fraudulent.

High returns that are too good to be true. The merchant card advance deal offered a 120% return, which is too good to be true. The promissory notes offered a 12-15% return (on the higher end of the spectrum, especially for the real estate deals). The distressed buy out deal offered 25% annual returns.

While I will not stand here and claim achieving high returns is impossible, it is (in my humble view) the outlier and not the norm...especially when the investment is being advertised as achieving such returns on a consistent basis (I painfully learned this lesson myself).

In addition, anyone in the business long enough has at some point experienced a downturn and potentially a loss. A seamless track record with zero history of losses (especially when lending!) is rare.

Ask for financials and understand the track record. Track record alone is not enough - think Bernie Madoff or the lessons learned from a past passive investment I was a part of (which subsequently turned out to be fraud). Those operators who have been in business for a while can provide long history of financials, preferably audited financials. You can start the review there and request ancillary reports, if pink flags appear or you have questions.

In the merchant card advances case the scheme ran for about a year, i.e., not long enough to establish a track record. So, if you are presented with a similar deal of a lifetime, give it at least two full years (though excessive returns alone would be a red flag).

Third party oversight by a reputable CPA firm (preferably one peer reviewed by the AICPA) adds additional comfort. This alone is not a guarantee to catch the fraud (the two multi-million-dollar fraud schemes I caught and saved those losses for my now former employer had been going on for years until I stepped in and stopped their music and one of them had a reputable CPA firm).

Glamorous lifestyle. In almost all cases, the criminal usually reroutes investor proceeds to maintain a lavish lifestyle – owning multiple luxury homes (or should I say mansions), flying first class, driving multiple Ferraris and Lamborghinis. Creating and maintaining such a lifestyle is not impossible but if one was to dig into the underlying business model and size up the margins, inevitably the question will arise – how is that lifestyle maintained given the profit profile of the business.

Paused or no communication. In almost all cases, communication stalled and eventually paused before the fall out. The LP forums were blowing up months before the Marco Santarelli's syndications with no word or response from the sponsor himself. In my case, I remember raising the red flag on this to the fund manager I invested with and on a well-known passive investor forum and in both cases my concerns were dismissed...This actually hurts more as these were the people I trusted and who were supposed to be fiduciaries, i.e., have investors' best interest at heart...

Trust your gut. While data and logic are important, so is your intuition. This fight or flight response that originates in the gut is difficult to explain. I can recall situations from my own past where I trusted my intuition and others where I did not. Hindsight is always 20-20 but if you catch yourself going back and forth too many times and ruminating, it is probably best to pause. Trust me - investment opportunities will be there, and it is better to miss on an outstanding one rather than enter into an outstandingly bad and painful one.

For better or worse, we learn most from our painful experiences, mistakes (which I like to call seminars) or the seminars of others. Thus, when I come across cases like this one, I like to dive in and see what new lessons I can extract and apply in my own investment journey. And I hope my reflections added value to you as well.

Whether through frameworks, personal experience, or market observations, the lesson is the same:

- Fraud rarely announces itself clearly
- Risk often hides behind familiarity and confidence
- And the cost of ignoring small red flags can be significant

The goal is not to become paranoid. The goal is to become disciplined.

Ask questions. Verify independently. And when something does not feel right, pause.

Because in investing, avoiding one bad deal often matters more than finding a great one.

PART 5

LEGAL STRUCTURES AND DOCUMENTS

CHAPTER 23

HOW TO INVEST (VIA WHAT ENTITY) IN A SYNDICATION AS A PASSIVE INVESTOR

A question I am frequently asked by passive investing partners is how (via what legal entity) they should invest in a syndication.

To begin with, I am not an attorney or a CPA and do not pretend to be either one. As such, my first response is typically that they should always consult their legal counsel and tax advisor.

However, below I share some of the more common ways I have seen passive investors enter into syndications and key considerations in relation to that.

Invest As an Individual Under One's Name

As passive investors do not actively manage the property, make key decisions, or run the business, they are shielded from liability (hence the term limited partners, LPs). As such, if there is a lawsuit, they are not part of that lawsuit – the property LLC and likely the management team would carry that liability instead. For that reason, most LPs enter into syndications under their individual name.

Invest Via a Business Entity

If asset protection or estate planning are important to an LP, then a Trust, Limited Partnership, or an LLC are some common business entities I see passive investors participate via. It is important to consult with your legal counsel and CPA to determine which structure is the most optimal one for you, keeping both asset protection and tax efficiency in mind.

Invest Via a Retirement Account Entity

Many passive investors prudently utilize their self-directed retirement accounts (see CHAPTER 30 for details on this) to invest in real estate. Depending on the self-directed provider and retirement account structure (IRA or Solo 401K), such retirement entity could be an LLC or a Trust. Sometimes the custodian may invest via their own entity. The set up varies quite a bit and is usually determined based on how the provider is organized and their requirements.

I understand the journey and process of investing in syndications can be overwhelming and confusing. I hope the above shed some light on this one common question I often discuss with passive investing partners and brings clarity to many.

CHAPTER 24

HOW TO READ A PRIVATE PLACEMENT MEMORANDUM LIKE A SEASONED INVESTOR

By the time you reach the Private Placement Memorandum (PPM), you have likely already reviewed the deal, listened to the sponsor, and decided that the investment may be a fit. Yet this is the stage where many investors shift into autopilot.

The document is long. It is written by attorneys. It is filled with legal and accounting terminology that can feel overwhelming.

So, most investors do one of two things. They either skim it or rely entirely on the sponsor's summary.

Both approaches create risk.

The PPM is not simply a formality. It is the document that governs your investment. It defines how decisions will be made, how cash will flow, what happens when things go right, and more importantly, what happens when things go wrong.

Over time, as I transitioned from reviewing deals as a lender to evaluating them as an investor, I began to read these documents differently. Not as a checklist, but as a way to understand alignment, incentives, and downside protection.

The goal of this chapter is to help you do the same.

What the PPM Is - And What It Is Not

The PPM is often misunderstood.

It is not a marketing document. That role belongs to the investment summary or pitch deck. It is also not designed to simplify the deal for you.

Instead, the PPM is a legal disclosure document. Its primary purpose is to outline the structure of the investment and disclose risks so the sponsor can comply with securities laws.

In other words, it is written to protect the issuer.

That does not make it unhelpful. In fact, it is one of the most important documents you will review. But it does mean you need to read it with the right lens.

You are not reading it to be persuaded. You are reading it to understand:

- How the deal actually works
- Where your rights begin and end
- How you are protected - or not protected

Understanding the Structure of the PPM Package

While investors often refer to everything collectively as the "PPM," what you are actually reviewing is a package of documents.

The Private Placement Memorandum itself typically includes an overview of the offering, key terms, and a detailed list of risk factors. It often mirrors what you have already seen in the investment presentation, but with more formal language.

However, the most important provisions are usually not in the narrative sections. They are embedded in the governing documents that accompany it.

The **Executive Summary** provides a high-level overview of the investment, including the property, the management team, target returns, and the business plan. It will largely mirror what was presented in the investor deck and is useful for confirming that the opportunity aligns with your investment criteria.

The **Summary of Terms** outlines the key economic and structural components of the deal. This includes ownership splits between LPs and GPs, minimum investment amounts, the sponsor's co-investment, distribution and capital event waterfalls, timing of distributions, and all applicable fees and expenses. This section is one of the most important, as it outlines in one to two pages how the entire investment is structured (similar to a bank term sheet or a letter of intent).

The **Risk Factors** section details the potential risks associated with the investment. It is often the longest and most intimidating part of the PPM. While many of these disclosures may appear broad, listing everything from market downturns to natural disasters, they should not be overlooked. Instead, they should serve as a starting point for discussions with the sponsor on how each risk is being mitigated. While many risks are standard, the way they are presented - and what is emphasized - can provide insight into how the sponsor is thinking about the investment. Strong operators are able to clearly articulate how they are addressing the risks outlined. That conversation is often more valuable than the language itself.

The **Operating Agreement** is where the real mechanics live. It outlines how decisions are made, how distributions are structured, how capital calls are handled, and what rights investors have.

The **Subscription Agreement** is where you formally commit to the investment, confirm your accreditation status, and agree to the terms. It is not uncommon for this section to also include the:

- **Investor Qualification Form** – where you will designate your investment/accreditation status. As discussed previously, for 506C investment opportunities, a third party will perform the investor accreditation status validation.
- **W-9 Form** – which you will complete for distributions and tax reporting purposes.
- **Signatures** – having read and understood everything, you sign, and you are now done!

There may also be an **Asset Management Agreement** that defines the responsibilities and compensation of the manager.

If there is ever a discrepancy between what was presented in the pitch deck and what is written in these documents, the legal documents will prevail. That is why this step in the process deserves careful attention.

Where Experienced LPs Actually Focus

A PPM can easily exceed 100 pages. Reading it line by line without a framework can feel overwhelming and, frankly, inefficient.

Experienced investors do not try to absorb everything equally. They focus on the sections that drive outcomes.

Over time, I have found that most of the meaningful risk and alignment comes down to a handful of areas.

How the Money Flows

The monetary rights sections spell out how (in what order) and when cash flow and capital are distributed, how the preferred return is structured, how profits are split between the general partner (GP) and limited partners (LPs), how *tax* benefits flow, and what the *sponsor fees* are, how they are structured, and when they are paid.

At the core of any syndication is the distribution structure. Not all structures are created equal.

Specifically, the distribution section will outline when distributions begin to accrue, how they will be handled (cumulative or cumulative and compounding or neither; return on capital or return of capital), and how the waterfall will flow (note that there is a cash flow waterfall and a capital event waterfall and they may not be the same).

Many deal structures today offer a preferred return (aka pref), a fixed % paid and based on the original principal investment amount until such principal is paid back in full. In a typical waterfall structure, such pref is paid before any profit splits kick in. The pref can be structured as follows:

- **Non-cumulative**, i.e., if the business did not generate sufficient profits to pay the pref, in part on in full, the unpaid pref is lost and will **not** be paid (least friendly)
- **Cumulative**, i.e., the unpaid pref is accrued and paid at the next capital event (most common)
- **Cumulative and compounding**, i.e., the unpaid pref is not only accrued, but also added to the principal investment amount and that new higher base is what subsequent prefs are based on **(most friendly)**

The most common distribution payouts are structured quarterly. However, **monthly** is more LP friendly.

It is also important to distinguish between distributions coming from actual operating cash flow versus those paid out of reserves or initial capital raised. The former reflects performance. The latter can create a false sense of stability.

The tax allocation will specify how profits and losses will flow as well as how any depreciation benefits will be allocated (e.g., based on cash contribution amount or percentage interests).

Lastly, the sponsor fees (such as acquisition fee, asset management fee, capital event fee, construction management fee, etc.) that are typically paid first before distributions are sent out, will also be clearly spelled out.

How Capital Calls Are Handled

Capital calls are one of the most important - and often overlooked - provisions. Note that in this specific section, I will reference capital calls in syndications. In the context of Funds (the section that follows) capital calls have a very different meaning, which we will dive into next.

In challenging environments, additional capital may be required to stabilize a property or protect the investment. The question is not whether this can happen. It is how it will be handled if it does (see CHAPTER 34 for a detailed overview on how to analyze a capital call).

In more LP-friendly structures, capital calls are optional, and investors who choose not to participate are diluted proportionally.

In less favorable scenarios, capital calls may be mandatory, or optional but accompanied by penalties beyond dilution. These structures can place investors in difficult positions, particularly during periods of market stress.

Understanding this provision upfront allows you to assess both your risk exposure and your flexibility if conditions change.

Who Controls the Decisions

As a passive investor, you are not involved in day-to-day operations. However, that does not mean governance is irrelevant.

The Operating Agreement will define what decisions the sponsor can make unilaterally and what requires investor approval. It will also outline whether investors have the ability to remove the manager under certain circumstances.

In some structures, LPs have meaningful protective rights and the ability to act in extreme situations. In others, control is heavily concentrated with the sponsor, with limited recourse for investors.

There is no single "correct" structure, but there should be alignment between the level of control and your level of trust in the operator.

In addition, it is important to consider **whether LPs have the ability to call a meeting** upon occurrence of material events and **how decisions will be made.** In that situation it is important to understand what type of vote would be required for a decision, as GPs are often investing 5-10% in their own deals, i.e., are part of the LP pool and may have the ability to influence the vote outcome.

Lastly, it is important to understand the notice periods (if any). This pertains to whether upon occurrence of certain events the sponsor is obligated to provide notice and if so, how much of a notice. Such terms could vary as follows:

- No notice (least friendly)
- Some notice
- 90-day notice (**most friendly**)

How Information Is Shared

Transparency is often overlooked until it becomes an issue.

The documents will outline how frequently investors receive updates, what financial information is provided, and when tax documents such as K-1s are delivered.

More investor-friendly structures provide clear expectations around reporting frequency and content. Others may include broader language that leaves reporting largely at the discretion of the sponsor.

While flexibility can be reasonable, lack of clarity can lead to misaligned expectations.

What Happens If You Want (or Need) to Exit

Syndications are illiquid by design. However, the extent of that illiquidity can vary.

The documents will specify whether interests can be transferred, whether the sponsor has a right of first refusal, and whether any redemption options exist.

In most cases, transfers require sponsor approval and may be difficult to execute. That is not inherently negative, but it reinforces the importance of entering these investments with an appropriate time horizon.

Reading Between the Lines: Alignment Over Optics

One of the biggest mistakes investors make is focusing only on headline terms.

A preferred return percentage, an equity split, or a projected IRR may look attractive on the surface. But the true quality of a deal lies in how those terms are structured beneath the surface.

Small differences in language can materially impact outcomes.

Is the preferred return cumulative or not?
Are capital calls optional or mandatory?
Do LPs have any meaningful voting rights?
Are fees aligned with performance or front-loaded?

These details may not stand out in a presentation, but they are clearly defined in the documents.

A Practical Approach to Reviewing the PPM

The goal is not to become an attorney or to memorize every clause.

It is to develop a structured approach.

Start by understanding how the deal is presented. Then move to how it is actually governed. Focus on how money flows, how decisions are made, and how downside scenarios are handled.

If something is unclear, ask questions. If something feels misaligned, trust that instinct and dig deeper.

And if the document feels overwhelming, you are not alone. Many investors choose to have an attorney review the documents and provide a summary of key terms. That can be a worthwhile investment, particularly for larger commitments.

Closing Thoughts

Over time, reading a PPM becomes less about decoding legal language and more about pattern recognition.

You begin to see how different structures impact outcomes. You recognize which terms are standard, which are investor-friendly, and which warrant further scrutiny.

That is when the shift happens.

You are no longer just participating in deals. You are evaluating them with intention.

And that is what ultimately separates a passive participant from a disciplined investor.

CHAPTER 25

FUNDS – DIVERSIFICATION, DELEGATION, AND THE TRADE-OFFS IN BETWEEN

Real Estate Funds vs Individual Investment Opportunities

As a passive investor, one is often faced with many investment choices. A common question I am often asked is whether it is better to invest in individual opportunities or in a fund. As with many things in real estate the answer is *it depends* on your own investment criteria and risk tolerance.

When investing in an **individual asset**, you can choose the market and the asset type/class. You will also receive a single K1. You will have one investment to track. All in all, it is simple. The downside of this approach is lack of diversification, which you can mitigate by making multiple investments in different markets or different asset classes or both. Over time this can result in higher administrative burden, both in investment tracking and number of K1s every tax season.

When investing in a **fund**, you depend on the operator to select the properties in the fund, which diversifies your exposure;

however, some of the assets may be across property classes or markets you are not fond of. You will still receive a single K1 from the fund but it may be more complex due to filing requirements in various states. Thus, this may or may not necessarily reduce your filing requirements for various states.

There is a variety of funds out there. (i) *Evergreen funds* that reinvest profits back into the fund. As an investor you have the ability to redeem shares (usually with a minimum notification period required and after a seasoning period; more often than not such redemptions are also usually capped and therefore, not guaranteed). (ii) *Open ended funds*, whereby returns are generated from the ongoing cash flow and investors can enter into and exit the fund at specific time frames defined by the sponsor. (iii) *Closed end funds*, whereby returns come from appreciation and the sale and no new money flows into the fund once it is closed. (iv) *Blind or semi blind funds* whereby you may know only one or two of the assets in the fund or none at all at the time of your initial investment, as those assets are acquired at a later point of time. (v) *Customizable funds* whereby you can choose the assets you invest in and may be able to contribute a smaller initial investment in each vs. the typical $50-100K minimum initial investment, i.e., you can spread your $50K investment across a couple of assets.

In some cases, the fund may invest as an LP and in others as a GP. There are also funds of funds whereby your fund sponsor may choose to participate in a bigger fund by bringing in a material portion of the proceeds via their fund.

As with traditional individual asset investments, vetting the fund manager is key (and even more important under the fund structure) as you also need to trust their own vetting process of the various sponsors/deals they choose to invest with/in.

In addition, one way to mitigate the risk of being under pressure to invest in borderline properties simply because you have money sitting in a fund, some sponsors may choose to pay small interest to their investors as a way to compensate them for tying up capital in the short run and introduce a bit more self-discipline while looking for a strong asset to invest in. Another way some funds manage the capital raising process is to only call the committed capital as/when it is needed or in pre-set stages/ timelines (aka capital call). Such capital calls are typical and not the same as the capital call referenced throughout this book for single-asset syndications.

Why Investing in A Fund May Make Sense for You?

Above I shared some of the unique aspects of investing in a fund relative to real estate individual syndications as well as key diligence points to consider when vetting a fund.

As I am often asked by investors on why it may make sense to invest in a fund, I will dive into this topic a bit more below.

There are three key advantages of investing via a fund structure:

1. Enhanced diversification.

Depending on the fund type (customizable vs. single asset class), one has the ability to diversify across a number of markets and operators. Proper diversification will depend on the fund manager's ability to source strong deals in strong markets with experienced operators and vet those investment opportunities via deep diligence. In recent years, the emergence of customizable funds or series funds has also enabled investors to pick and choose their own individual deals via a single fund structure offered by the fund manager.

When it comes to real estate, I believe in being a subject matter expert.

2. More efficient reporting.

Getting hundreds of pages of K1 reports during tax season can be overwhelming. It is also difficult to control the timing of each K1. In a fund structure, investors will usually receive a single K1 that will capture all assets held in the fund. Similarly, monthly/quarterly reports can be consolidated into a single one (while still showing property level details for those who like to peel the onion a few layers deep). Report consolidation becomes especially important as individual investors start growing their portfolios, where managing multiple reports and reporting deadlines can become administratively burdensome pretty quickly.

3. Special conditions/terms.

When investing via a fund, one may be able to enter into marquee deals at a lower minimum required investment amount (e.g., $50-100K vs. $100-250K). In addition, one may be able to benefit from special terms, such as higher preferred return of 8% (vs. 7%) or more favorable carried interest of 80% LP – 20% GP (vs. 70% LP – 30% GP). All of that is contingent on the size of the fund, the fund manager's ability to negotiate more favorable terms with the operators (in exchange for coming in with a single large investment), and the operator's willingness to offer better terms (in exchange for having a single large check investor – the fund – vs having to work with multiple retail investors). Depending on the deal size, this may be more favorable for the retail investors. A prime example is Ray Dalio's Bridgewater Associates $100BN+ fund, which is one of the largest hedge funds in the space and its minimum investment is $7.5BN+. Its investors are typically large institutions and pension funds who are able to write that check, typically that funds for which they raised from high-net-worth individuals and family offices, etc. by allowing lower minimums (e.g., $500K).

Being able to take advantage of the fund benefits above is contingent on your confidence in the fund manager's track record of finding strong deals with proven operators and having a sound vetting process to minimize overall risk and achieve optimal returns.

Five Key Points to Keep in Mind When Vetting Funds

There has been a large increase in funds over the past few years, as many professionals in the real estate syndication space transition from co-Manager (aka co-GP) structures to fund structures. There are many (very good) reasons why an investor may choose to make that transition. Above I discussed the various funds and fund structures. Below I'll offer five key areas you as a passive investor can focus on to perform diligence on funds and fund managers.

1. Understand what specific diligence the fund manager does upfront.

The benefits of investing via a fund were discussed above. However, the fund structure introduces an important shift. Rather than selecting individual deals yourself, you are delegating that responsibility to the fund manager. As a result, your focus should shift toward understanding and validating *their* investment and diligence process.

Key questions to consider include:

- What level of background checks are performed on sponsors? Are these comprehensive investigations or surface-level screenings?
- How is the underlying asset evaluated - market, financials, and business plan?
- What diligence is conducted on the sponsor's track record and execution capabilities?
- How rigorously are deal structures and underwriting assumptions reviewed?

A disciplined fund manager should be able to clearly articulate their process and provide examples of how they have applied it in practice.

2. Understand how the fund manager monitors the investment performance.

Once the deal closes, the real work of executing on the business plan begins. And while the fund manager will typically not be involved in the day-to-day operations, it is important to understand what systems and processes they have in place to monitor the investment performance and stay ahead of any potential issues. They should be able to share specific reports and examples of such. At the end of the day, the fund manager still has fiduciary responsibility towards its investors.

3. Understand what levers of influence the fund manager has on the syndicator (if any).

While a fund would typically join a syndication as a limited partner, i.e., a passive investor and as such, the fund itself will NOT be involved in the day-to-day operations, funds typically bring a single but very large seven or eight figure check into a deal. Thus, it is not unreasonable to expect the fund manager to have some influence on the syndicators. Depending on the size of their participation into the deal, they may or may not have voting rights but will and should have some level of influence as well as ability to sit in on asset management calls or other meetings open to the managers and general partners. This becomes particularly important during periods of distress when timely communication, visibility, and ability to provide feedback are key.

4. Understand the source of funds of the fund.

Many funds in the traditional multifamily syndication world would be solely funded by the equity (or in other words - private investors' capital). However, it is not uncommon (especially in the debt fund space) for the fund to take on leverage (aka debt). There are lenders and non-financial institutions who would lend to the fund based on the capital commitments and other factors. As we have learned in prior snippets, leverage tends to enhance returns (as it uses other people's money). Taking on leverage, however, also increases the level of risk. This is why, when evaluating funds and their proforma returns, it is important to understand their source of funds and then determine if the structure aligns with your risk tolerance.

5. Gain comfort with the fund managers communication and track record.

Similar to a typical syndication structure, communication throughout the tenor of the investment is key for transparency and information purposes. You want to understand how and how frequently the fund manager communicates and what type of reporting they request and receive from the syndicator. They should be able to share examples of both with you, so you can decide if the level of detail and frequency is in line with your expectations. Furthermore, you want to gain comfort with their track record and ability to select well performing investments. While they may not have a 100% batting average, what I would typically look for is consistency and overall performance over a longer period of time.

Bonus Tip:

Not all funds are created equal in terms of the fee structure. Therefore, it is important to understand how the manager gets compensated, how such compensation impacts the fund's and passive investors' projected returns, and if alignment of interests exists.

There are of course many more questions to ask upfront when vetting a fund and a fund manager. I shared some of those above and I'm happy to speak with you further, if you'd like to explore the topic in more detail.

PART 6

TAXES AND TAX DEFERRAL STRATEGIES

CHAPTER 26

TAX DEFERRAL - REALITY VS MYTH / TAX DEFERRAL BENEFITS AND WATCH OUTS

I mentioned earlier the tax deferral benefits of investing in real estate. Tom Wheelwright's last book The Win-Win Wealth Strategy does a great job explaining why the government has created such incentives and how they benefit not only the real estate investor and the community, but also the government itself. Herein I will scratch the surface of a few of those tax deferral benefits. As usual, I would emphasize that it is best to and you should always consult with your CPA on any additional strategies and if/how any of the ones noted herein can apply to you. Let's dive in!

1. Depreciation.

Depreciation is a non-cash expense. The underlying premise is that the building loses its book value over time due to natural wear and tear. We know this is really not the case (as the property's market value, especially when held long term, usually increases over time). Each time a property is sold, the new owner restarts the clock on such depreciation. However, this non-cash expense can reduce the net income generated by such property and thereby reduce its taxable income.

A commercial property is usually depreciated over a 39-year straight-line period. A residential property (multifamily is included in such definition for tax purposes) depreciates over a 27.5-year straight line period.

The tax code also allows an owner to accelerate the depreciation and record it in year 1 of owning the property by performing a cost segregation study. Such study is conducted by property engineers and tax professionals who detail each component of a building. Such component may be on a different depreciation schedule, i.e., some components may be depreciated over 5 years vs. 27.5 years. This process in essence allows one to accelerate the depreciation on average. Currently (as of the time of writing this book) one can claim 100% bonus depreciation (unless the tax code is changed again).

When (bonus) depreciation is taken, it can create paper losses. Such passive losses can be used to offset other passive income. This can potentially offset a big portion of your taxable income if you or your spouse qualify as a real estate professional "REPS" (see more on REPS below). If you earn $250K or above, your passive losses can only offset other passive income (e.g., passive losses from a cost segregation on a new deal in Year 1, can offset passive income on another deal that is now in Year 2 or 3). In addition, even if you have no other passive income to offset, you do not lose such passive losses. These losses are accumulated and can later be applied against the gain on sale of the asset.

Depreciation serves as a tax deferral strategy. Deferral vs. savings is a more accurate way to describe it, as **it is usually**

recaptured at the time of sale (irrespective of whether you claimed it or not).

At the time of recapture Section 1245 is recaptured first. This is all personal property that was accelerated with bonus depreciation in the cost seg. That portion is taxed at ordinary income tax rates.

Next is Section 1250, which is a mix of ordinary income and 25% flat tax rates (this is why working with a real-estate savvy CPA is important to determine the tax impact specific to you).

The remaining portion is usually taxed at the capital gains tax rate (as of the time of writing this book such tax rate is 15-20% for long-term capital gains, depending on your marital status and income level).

2. 1031 Exchange.

1031 is a section within the IRS code that allows one to exchange one property for another (of equal or greater value) and thereby defer the tax on the gain from the sale. One can 1031 exchange properties indefinitely, until one passes away, at which point title would transfer to one's successor at a market (vs. cost) basis (aka step up basis) minimizing the successor's tax liability should they choose to sell. The replacement property must be identified within 45 days from and the exchange must close within 180 days from when the relinquished property closes the sale.

1031 may not make sense in all scenarios. For example, if you have meaningful passive losses accumulated over time, they may be sufficient to offset most of the capital gains and depreciation recapture, making the cost and time of a 1031 exchange not as attractive.

If you decide to proceed with a 1031 exchange, you must engage a qualified intermediary to manage the exchange and before you take any action, as always you should consult with your CPA to determine the optimal strategy for your individual situation.

I will cover 1031 Exchanges in syndications later in CHAPTERS 27-28.

3. Real Estate Professional Status (REPS, REP) and Material Participation

A REP spends: (i) more than 750 hours per year on a real estate business (e.g., an active investor would qualify as one but an admin working in a title company would likely not) **and** (ii) more than 50% of the time on a real estate business. The 50% rule makes it difficult for a full time W2 earner to qualify as a REP as it is generally very difficult to prove that you work more than 40 hours a week on the real estate business in addition to your full-time job. You must track your hours and be able to clearly document what you did and when, in the event of an audit. The type of activity (e.g., material participation or not, see the REPS section of this chapter re this further down below), is also an important factor to determine if one can turn the passive losses into active losses. The benefit of being able to qualify as REPS is overall reduction in your tax bracket to as low as 15% (vs. 35%).

4. Cash out refinance tax free income.

When you refinance a property, such cash out refinance income is usually tax free as the source of that income is debt (you are leveraging your property even more). Debt is not considered earned or investment income for tax purposes. This is one of the powers of real estate – when you own an asset you can keep refinancing every few years and utilize the cash out income to invest in more income producing assets.

5. Rental income and capital gains tax.

As rental income is not earned W2 income, it is not subject to Social Security and Medicare tax. In addition, while short-term capital gains (e.g., when flipping properties) are taxed as ordinary earned income (and therefore would fall in the various ordinary income tax brackets), if you hold a property long term (more than a year), the gains on sale are considered long-term capital gains and as such, taxed at a lower income tax rate (15-20%, depending on your tax bracket). As noted above, you must work with a qualified CPA as the depreciation recapture and capital gains flow through a variety of buckets, each one taxed differently.

The above strategies are just a few ways to reduce or defer one's taxes and designed to stimulate investment in real estate. As noted previously, it is always best to consult with your CPA to explore additional paths that may be more applicable to your individual situation and goals.

How Can K1 Losses Offset Your Income? Or Can They?

One question I am frequently asked is how such paper loss is treated and whether it can offset one's active income.

As usual the answer is - it depends. And as usual, **please consult with your CPA or tax advisor as the below snippet is not intended to serve as tax advice.**

For those that are actively participating in the management of real estate, i.e., making management decisions such as lease renewal terms, tenant approvals, expense approvals, etc., the IRS has certain provisions. Specifically, if one makes below $100,000 in annual adjusted gross income (AGI), you can use up to $25,000 of passive losses to offset against the active income. Such allowance phases out at 50% up to AGI of $150,000 and above $150,000 it completely phases out.

For example, if you make up to $90,000 in AGI, you could apply the full $25,000 against the W2 income. If your income is $125,000, then you can offset up to $12,500 [=$25,000-(($125,000-$100,000) *50%)]. And at $150,000, it is $0.

What happens if you do not have a rental portfolio or are not involved in the management decisions and are truly passive? You do NOT lose such passive losses. Instead, you can either carry them forward to offset the capital gain and depreciation recapture at the time of sale OR you can apply them to offset other passive income.

Many people apply this strategy when they implement what is known as a "**lazy 1031 exchange**", i.e., in the year when they record a gain from the sale of a syndicated property, they enter into another syndication expected to perform cost segregation and thereby record a large paper loss in the same tax year. Thus, the tax loss in year 1 of the new syndication offsets (partially or fully) the gain recorded from the prior syndication.

When investing in multifamily, where the property size is larger, such paper losses can be pretty meaningful (especially if your ownership share is larger). Such tax deferral and tax savings can be potentially used to invest in other cash flowing investments thereby augmenting one's income stream and net worth over time … step by step, year over year… Time does wonders in real estate, if one is patient.

CHAPTER 27

ADDITIONAL TAX DEFERRAL STRATEGIES FOR REAL ESTATE UNVEILED

Tax deferral is one of the aspects of real estate investing that make it a powerful wealth building vehicle. Tax is ultimately due at some point of time. However, the ability to defer such liability carries the power of the time value of money, i.e., the proceeds one would otherwise pay in tax can be deployed towards cash flowing investments generating returns in the interim.

As usual, before exploring any tax deferral strategy you must consult with your CPA and tax advisor to determine the most optimal path for you.

Below I reveal some of the most commonly used strategies and provide a high-level comparative chart in the end.

1031 Exchange

1031 is a section within the IRS code that ultimately allows one to defer the qualifying gains from sale of a property. However, for that deferral to be recognized, the investor must follow a few strict guidelines.

- A qualified intermediary must be engaged. And one should also involve his/her CPA.
- One has 45 days to identify a replacement property from the day one closes on the sale of the relinquished property and 180 days to close on the replacement property. The 180-day clock starts ticking from the sale date or the due date of the tax return for the tax year during which the relinquished property was sold.
- The exchange must be like for like, i.e., real estate for real estate, not real estate into an LLC owning RE (in some states exchanging mineral rights into real estate might be eligible).
- The qualifying property must be held for investment – intent matters.
- The replacement property must be of equal or greater value. There are specific reinvestment requirements to follow.
- The exchange MUST be set up BEFORE the sale of the relinquished property (before the PSA is signed).
- Typical exit is a sale of the property or 1031 exchange into another property, which 1031 exchange process can continue indefinitely until one passes away at which point the property passes on to one's heirs on a step-up tax basis.

Tenant In Common (TIC)

This vehicle offers the ability to 1031 exchange a property into a syndication. However, the syndication must have the TIC structure set up ahead of time. Not all sponsors offer that structure as it requires additional set up from a legal standpoint. Such set up, if not done correctly could also trigger a tax liability and void the 1031 exchange altogether. It can also result in complications around voting power, control, fees, and profit splits. For that reason, many sponsors would have minimum required investment amounts that start at $500K-$1MM in order to accept 1031 exchange investors.

Delaware Statutory Trusts

Delaware Statutory Trust (not to be confused with Deferred Sale Trust) became popular since 2004 and represents another tax deferral vehicle. It represents fractional ownership in a Trust that owns the underlying real estate.

- The Trust holds title to real property (most common investments are multifamily or NNN leased retail or office but may include other commercial real estate like self-storage, senior living, retail, etc.)
- DSTs typically obtain low LTV (50% + or -) non-recourse financing
- Can close within five days from submission of subscription documents
- The typical investments are safer well maintained low capex need assets. Given the lower risk, returns are also lower.
- No K1 is issued at year end – only an operating statement with your pro rata ownership share, which document your CPA can input into Schedule E of your tax return
- Only available to accredited investors

- You relinquish control to the DST sponsor/operator who will operate the property. As such, DST investments are considered passive in nature.
- No future contributions of capital are allowed – e.g., for capex so the sponsor must raise upfront and estimate well. And even then, no heavy capex is allowed, only routine and typical repair and maintenance.
- No refinance or re-borrow of new funds and no new investors are allowed, i.e., no new capital infusions post close.
- Excess cash must be distributed.
- No 1031 exchange into another DST is allowed as it is no longer like for like – may be able to sell your share to other DST trustees
- Typical exits include a sale to a REIT, institutional buyers, high net worth 1031 exchange buyers, or a Sec 721 exchange into a REIT.
- Key players – your CPA, DST sponsor/operator, licensed broker dealers selling the DST, provides immediate access to properties to 1031 exchange into
- Potential to diversify into various properties
- Small min amount of $100K

Deferred Sales Trusts

The Deferred Sales trust is a form of installment sale. One would sell the property to a trust (managed by a third party on the seller's behalf), which then sells the property to the final buyer.

- The trust then pays you the proceeds from sale over an extended period of time (up to 20 or more years).

- Only the installments are taxed, which allows you to spread out the tax liability over time.
- Excess funds not yet distributed can be invested in other low risk investments or treasuries, generating additional income.
- Ensure you are working with an experienced professional in that matter – tax & legal – to set it up properly.
- The set up and maintenance fees could be significant. As such (and as with any other major ticket decision), a cost (set up and maintenance fees) vs. the benefit (tax savings over time) should help one assess this option.

Opportunity Zones (OZs)

Investments in OZ are typically in distressed zones or communities who would benefit from investment in the region. As such, these investments enjoy a preferred tax treatment.

- The capital gain portion of a sale (not the full sale proceeds) can be invested into a Qualified Opportunity Fund and deferred.
  - Per the IRS: "Gains that may be deferred are called "eligible gains." They include both capital gains and qualified 1231 gains, but only gains that would be recognized for federal income tax purposes before January 1, 2027, and that are not from a transaction with a related person. For you to obtain this deferral, the amount of the eligible gain must be timely invested in a QOF in exchange for an equity interest in the QOF (qualifying investment). Once you have done this, you can claim the deferral on your federal

income tax return for the taxable year in which the gain would be recognized if you do not defer it."

- If the Opportunity Zone investment is held for at least 10 years, investors may elect to step up the basis of the OZ investment to fair market value upon exit, effectively eliminating capital gains tax on the appreciation of the OZ investment itself.
- You may defer the gain in whole or in part.
- No intermediary is required.
- A taxpayer has 180 days from the date of the sale or exchange of appreciated property to invest the realized capital gain dollars into a Qualified Opportunity Fund
- The 180-day period during which to invest in a Qualified OZ Fund begins on the day the installment payment is received, even if the installment sale giving rise to the gain took place prior to December 2017.
    - If your installment sale took place after 2017, if you elect installment treatment for your sale, you have two options for how to defer gain detailed here (https://www.wellsfargo.com/the-private-bank/insights/planning/wpu-qualified-opportunity-zones/)
- The deferral expires on December 31, 2026, at which point the deferred gains become taxable under current law. However, proposed legislation (including the One Big Beautiful Bill introduced in 2025) contemplates extending or modifying the Opportunity Zone program, though as of this writing, no extension has been finalized.

- There is no requirement for like kind property.
- The original step-up in basis benefits (10% and 15%) are no longer available due to timing constraints relative to the December 31, 2026 deferral deadline. Future legislation, including proposals under the One Big Beautiful Bill (2025), may reintroduce or modify these incentives, but they are not currently in effect.

While not yet finalized, proposed updates to the Opportunity Zone program may include:

1. Extension of the deferral period beyond 2026
1. Reintroduction of basis step-up incentives
1. Refinement of eligible zones and reporting requirements
1. Increased focus on measurable community impact

Investors should treat these as potential enhancements rather than guaranteed benefits and underwrite investments based on current law.

Other

There are a few other vehicles one can utilize such as foundations, charitable remainder trusts, spendthrift trusts, and installment sales/seller finance.

Which option is the best really depends on one's personal situation and goals around timing, comfort with relinquishing control, desired deferral timelines. As such, you should always discuss such events with your tax advisor and CPA.

Exhibit 11: Comparative Summary

	1031 Exchange	Delaware Statutory Trusts	Deferred Sales Trust	Opportunity Zones	TIC
Timelines	45 days from sale of the relinquished property to identify a new one and 180 days to close	No	No	180 days from the last day of the tax year in which the sale occurred or the date of sale	45 days from sale of the relinquished property to identify a new one and 180 days to close
Party To Loan Agreement	Yes	No	No	No	No
Recourse/Personal Liability	Yes	No	No	No	Maybe
Involvement in day to the day operations	Yes	No	No	No	Maybe
Project Duration	Could be forever until the next 1031 exchange	5-10 years	could be 20 years (or more)	Varies	3-7 years
Third Parties Involved	Yes - must work with a qualified intermediary (QI)	Yes - DST broker and DST sponsor	Trust	Deal sponsor (no QI is required)	Deal sponsor
Control	Yes	No	No	No	No
Performance/Sponsor Risk	No sponsor risk as you retain control	Yes	No	Yes	Yes
Fees	No, other than to QI	Commissiosn, broker dealer fees, management fees	Set up an maintenance fees, could be steep (.5% of the asset's value of the first $1 million and 1.25% of anything over $1 million.)	Acquisition fee, asset management fee, other fees may apply too	Acquisition fee, asset management fee, other fees may apply too

Sources:

Lifetime tax Free Wealth by Dave Foster

An Introduction to DST Properties For 1031 Exchange Investors by Dwight Kay

Wells Fargo Private Bank publication 10-2022

CHAPTER 28

1031 EXCHANGE IN SYNDICATIONS

I am often asked how one can 1031 exchange a property they own into a syndication. This tax deferral strategy while common for properties you own 100% is a bit more complex and not as common in the real estate syndication space. However, it can be done.

In order to 1031 exchange into a syndication, the sponsor would typically have to set up a Tenant In Common (TIC) structure. The TIC structure means that all TIC members have joint and several ownership with equal control.

Typically, the sponsors have control over the deal and would not want to relinquish dayto-day management decisions or voting power to a passive investor who may or may not have the experience relevant for managing the subject property and executing on the business plan. There may be a way to structure around the management and voting power of the TIC owners (e.g., via a side letter). However, as always it is best to consult with your syndication and real estate attorney as well as a tax advisor on how to approach this. It is important that the structure is both IRS and SEC compliant.

In addition, depending on the ownership share, lenders would do due diligence on and may also underwrite the TIC owners. This involves running their credit reports and background checks as well as requesting their personal financial statements and real estate schedules.

Keeping up with the 1031 exchange deadlines noted above coupled with the additional legal paperwork and lender requirements makes it costly and requires additional work, legal fees, and effort. Therefore, it is not uncommon for sponsors to require higher investment minimums for 1031 exchange investors – e.g., $500K - $1MM or more.

For an existing syndication and assuming all owners (GPs and LPs) agree to it, it is also possible to perform a 1031 exchange into a new syndication. As usual one must consult with the qualified intermediary (the one in charge of handling the 1031 exchange to ensure it complies with all requirements), your CPA, and your attorney to ensure one avoids any pitfalls.

CHAPTER 29

WHAT IS A REAL ESTATE PROFESSIONAL AND WHY DOES IT MATTER TO YOU?

I previously discussed the various tax deferral benefits of real estate investing. Below I will dive into one of those in more detail – real estate professional status (aka REP or REPS). **As always, before taking any steps, please consult with your CPA.**

Earlier in the chapter I discussed the concept of depreciation, how it results in paper/tax losses, which one can deduct against taxable income (typically against other passive income).

You can generally deduct up to $25,000 in passive losses against your ordinary income (W2 wages) if your modified adjusted gross income (MAGI) is $100,000 or less. This deduction phases out by $1 for every $2 of MAGI above $100,000, until $150,000 when it is completely phased out. This is where REPS can be beneficial.

REPS effectively enables a qualified individual to apply real estate losses against one's income.

To achieve a REP status, one must spend: (i) more than 750 hours per year on a real estate business, (ii) more than 50% of the time on a real estate business AND more than anyone else. The 50% rule makes it difficult for a full time W2 earner to qualify as a REP as it is generally very difficult to prove that you work more than 40 hours a week on the real estate business in addition to your full-time job. You must track your hours and be able to clearly document activity, in the event of an audit.

For more details on REPS and REPS qualifications, you can check out the IRS guidance here (https://www.irs.gov/forms-pubs/about-publication-925).

To be able to apply real estate losses against one's taxable income one should be able to prove not only a REP status **but also material participation in the trade or business**.

The benefit of being able to qualify as REPS and **material participation** is overall reduction in your tax bracket to as low as 15% (vs. 35%). Whether you are single individual or filing jointly, this can be meaningful.

For a couple with high combined W2 wages or other high-income earners in general, the tax deferral or tax savings can be impactful. For example, if you make say $250K/ year and your spouse manages the real estate investment portfolio full time and generates $100K in passive losses due to cost segregation, depreciation, or other tax deferral strategies, your joint household income reduces from $250K to $150K, putting your family in a lower tax bracket.

Which one of you becomes a REP will depend on your individual income levels, career trajectory and job satisfaction, and passion about real estate. Perhaps your roles are already somewhat defined or perhaps one of you already works part-time and therefore being able to dedicate the additional time required to manage the real estate business. Whatever your circumstances, the spouse who will manage the real estate portfolio will in effect run a business.

I hope this section provided food for thought and that it at least suggested questions and discussion topics you can bring up next time you meet with your CPA to determine if and how they could apply to your individual situation.

CHAPTER 30

HOW TO USE YOUR RETIREMENT ACCOUNT TO INVEST IN REAL ESTATE (A BALANCED VIEW)

I often receive a surprised look when I mention to people that they can use their retirement account to invest in real estate. A follow up question often then raised (with some skepticism) is - why is that not so widely talked about or promoted? For one simple reason, traditional employer 401Ks and traditional retirement account providers (IRA, Roth IRA, Rollover IRA) are provided by traditional brokerage firms who mostly benefit from managing stocks, bonds, and mutual fund investments and do not get compensated for investing in real estate, commodities, crypto, mortgage notes or other types of investments (new regulation is in process, which will enable access to alternative investments, including real estate; however, it is not in effect as of the time of writing this book).

It was only after I started building my real estate portfolio that I learned about self-directed retirement accounts. The two more popular options today include self-directed Solo 401K and SDIRA (self-directed IRA).

A self-directed retirement plan is exactly that - a retirement account that allows you to self-direct or choose what type of investment you want in addition to stocks, bonds, and mutual funds.

Before we dive into investing into syndications via a self-directed retirement account, it is imperative that you get familiarized with the compliance requirements pertaining to those. Not following such requirements can trigger a taxable event and blow up your entire retirement account. As this book is not intended to serve as a detailed tutorial on self-directed retirement account, you are welcome to message me and I can share a few good educational resources on the topic.

How do I establish a self-directed retirement plan? The account would typically be established by a self-directed retirement account custodian (I can provide a list of providers you can look into to start your search with; working with a custodian can be especially helpful, if you are not familiar with the regulatory requirements as they can help guide you to ensure the account remains both compliant and the tax-deferral status is protected). In addition, if you are switching jobs or leaving your job, you would be eligible to roll over your employer sponsored 401K plan proceeds into a self-directed retirement account. **There are some procedural steps you must follow in order to avoid triggering a tax event** but with the guidance of the retirement account provider, it can be easily accomplished. This rollover process could take up to two weeks depending on the incumbent provider.

The key differences between the Self-Directed Solo 401K and the SDIRA pertain to checkbook control, amount of maximum contribution allowed, and other tax and debt related advantages noted below, detailed below.

What are the different self-directed retirement account types?

Not all are created equal! Such accounts come in all shapes and forms and which one suits you best depends on:

Your Desire for Control (hands on vs hands off):

If you are looking to be more hands on, then a custodian managed account may be a better fit for you, where all investments will go through the custodian for review and compliance approval and they will also help with the annual compliance filings.

If you are more hands off and familiar with the self-dealing limitations, then a self-managed account may be a better fit for you.

Your Personal Situation (employed vs self-employed):

If you are employed or do not have a side hustle, then likely your only option is a retirement account.

However, if you are self-employed or have a fee income side hustle, then you have the option to start your own solo 401K plan (which also helps avoid UDFI tax, more on that below).

Lastly, a self-directed account with brokerage firms like Vanguard/Fidelity/Schwab is NOT the same, as they typically limit investments to stocks/bonds/mutual funds and would NOT allow you to invest in alternative assets.

Other Considerations

Checkbook control: In a Solo 401K you or your company (if you are self-employed) may serve as the trustee and as such, you have 100% checkbook control of the plan. In a SDIRA you must work through a custodian who will administer the account on your behalf.

Amount of maximum allowed contribution: That amount varies from year to year. For 2026 it is $72,000 (or $80,000, if 50 years or older) for a Solo 401K (this includes elective and profit-sharing contributions combined) and $7,500 for SDIRA (or $8,600, if 50 years old or older).

Other tax advantages of a Solo 401K vs IRA: What many people do not know is that certain income streams may be taxed while in a SDIRA. The two most common ones are **UBIT** (unrelated business income tax) and **UDFI** (unrelated debt financed income, a type of UBIT). **UBIT** would apply if you are actively (vs. passively) involved in managing the real estate investment. That tax rate could be 35% or more. As such, you may want to apply SDIRA proceeds towards passive investments like syndications for example. **UDFI** is incurred when the property purchased is financed and such tax is based on the highest amount of leverage carried within the last 12 months. For example, if you bought a property in Year 1 for $100K and financed it at a 50% LTV with non-recourse debt and you sell the property for $200K in Year 5, then 50% of the profit or $50K would be subject to UBIT. That taxable income is before any adjustments for depreciation recapture, etc. There may be certain exceptions to that, if the debt is paid off early. As such, you should always consult with your real estate savvy CPA to assess the tax impact based on your specific situation and specific investment and how best to approach it or time the sale.

The Solo401K is exempt from UDFI but may not be exempt from UBIT, if you are actively involved in the investment.

A quick back of the envelope calculation of UDFI is:

1. Take the income generated from the property, say hypothetically it is $100K.
2. Apply the loan to value ratio. Let's say it is 55%.
3. The income subject to UDFI would be 55% x $100K = $55K
4. Apply any deductions applicable to the property (that number is typically not known until taxes are filed). Let's assume for now it is $30K.
5. That leaves $25K (=$55K-$30K) subject to the UDFI tax, which is published in IRS form 990W

Exhibit 12:

2022 Tax Rate Schedule for Trusts

If the amount on Form 990-W, line 1, is: Over—	*But not over—*	*Enter on line 2:*	*Of the amount over—*
$-0-	$2,750	10%	$-0-
2,750	9,850	$275.00 + 24%	$2,750
9,850	13,450	1,979.00 + 35%	9,850
13,450	------	3,239.00 + 37%	13,450

6. So, in our hypothetical example above, the number would be $3,239 + 37% x ($25K-$13.45K) = $7,512, which UDFI tax would be paid out of the IRA.

7. If depreciation and other deductions exceed income, which they often do in Year 1 and 2, the number would be lower and potentially $0. And needless to say, the above will factor in your share of the investment only (vs. the total deal as you do not own 100% of the deal).
8. **I would strongly recommend leaning on your CPA to calculate this number and to complete the appropriate filings**, as neither you, nor I are tax professionals and while I have good general understanding, I am not a certified CPA or tax advisor and I will **not** pretend to be one.

Other features: In case of emergency, you are able to take a loan against your Solo401K in the amount of the lesser of $50K or 50% of the vested balance. The loan should generally be repaid within five years and must charge a reasonable interest rate. The SDIRA does not offer that benefit.

The above information just scratches the surface of the self-directed options and how they can be utilized. I definitely recommend that you connect with one of the self-directed account providers and your CPA, if you choose to dive deeper into this.

CHAPTER 31

THE PASSIVE INVESTOR'S GUIDE TO UNDERSTANDING THE K1S

There is this time of the year...once a year...every year... when you feverishly scramble to put the package together and then await the outcome and score on how well you did and either pay up if you were naughty or get paid if you were nice! No, I am not talking about Santa Claus and Christmas. ☺ Even though they are somewhat alike, I am referring to annual tax filing season when you scramble to put together the reporting package for your CPA and anxiously await the outcome – will you receive a refund or will you have to pay?

If you are investing passively, you have hopefully selected an investment with a cost segregation feature that would have the ability to bring forward a substantial amount of the depreciation in year one to effectively defer taxes. But how do you know how you did? And how do you navigate through the complexities of reading the K1 you receive from the sponsors.

Below I will demystify just that. Needless to say, I'd be sharing a general example, i.e., as always **you must consult with your CPA and tax advisor re your individual situation**.

To begin with, let's take a step back and clarify what the K1 is. Typically, entities with more than one partner complete form 1065, or a partnership tax return. The K1 form is part of that return and reflects your share of the partnership activity. The partnership itself does not pay taxes. The partners do, based on their individual share.

Part 1 of the K1 will typically list the partnership entity. In a syndication, this would be the entity you are a member of.

Exhibit 13:

Part I	Information About the Partnership
A	Partnership's employer identification number
B	Partnership's name, address, city, state, and ZIP code
C	IRS center where partnership filed return: e-file
D	☐ Check if this is a publicly traded partnership (PTP)

Part 2 will show your individual information.

It is important to review and double check it for accuracy. Specifically, you want to ensure that **Clauses E and F**, i.e., the entity information and TIN are correct if you are investing via a legal entity (or your name and SSN, if investing as an individual).

Clause J will reflect your investment share as % of the total partnership.

Clause K will show your share of the debt, to the extent you are one of the signers and/or guarantors on the loan.

Clause L will show your principal investment amount, which amount will/should match your principal investment. For example, if you invested $100K, it will be shown there. Your current year loss will be reflected here too, thereby arriving at your ending capital account balance. This balance is one you want to track closely over the lifecycle of the deal. It will ultimately show the capital payable to you at the conclusion of the deal.

Lastly, if you are investing via a retirement account, **Part 2 I2** box will be checked.

Exhibit 14:

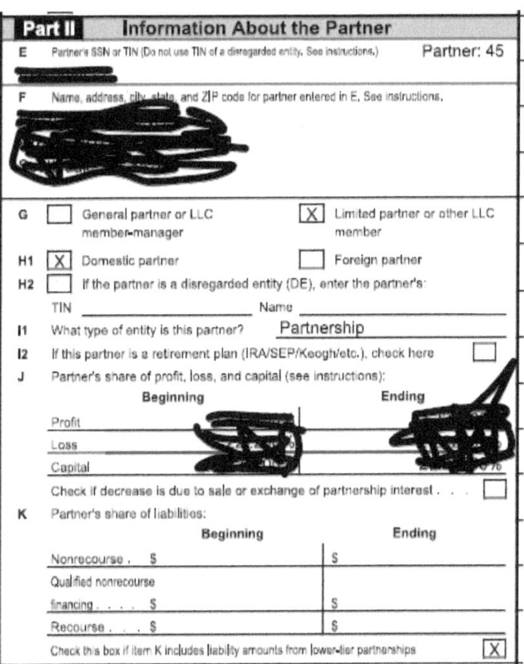

Part II Information About the Partner

E Partner's SSN or TIN (Do not use TIN of a disregarded entity. See instructions.) Partner: 45

F Name, address, city, state, and ZIP code for partner entered in E. See instructions.

G ☐ General partner or LLC member-manager ☒ Limited partner or other LLC member

H1 ☒ Domestic partner ☐ Foreign partner

H2 ☐ If the partner is a disregarded entity (DE), enter the partner's:

TIN ______ Name ______

I1 What type of entity is this partner? Partnership

I2 If this partner is a retirement plan (IRA/SEP/Keogh/etc.), check here ☐

J Partner's share of profit, loss, and capital (see instructions):

	Beginning	Ending
Profit		
Loss		
Capital		

Check if decrease is due to sale or exchange of partnership interest . . . ☐

K Partner's share of liabilities:

	Beginning	Ending
Nonrecourse . . $		$
Qualified nonrecourse financing . . . . $		$
Recourse . . . $		$

Check this box if item K includes liability amounts from lower-tier partnerships ☒

Exhibit 15:

L	Partner's Capital Account Analysis	
	Beginning capital account	$
	Capital contributed during the year . .	$
	Current year net income (loss)	$
	Other increase (decrease) (attach explanation)	$
	Withdrawals and distributions	$ ( )
	Ending capital account	$
M	Did the partner contribute property with a built-in gain (loss)? ☐ Yes ☒ No If "Yes," attach statement. See instructions.	

Part 3 will show your share of the income and loss and any other income. Items 1 shows non-rental income (e.g., lending), 2 - rental real estate income, 3- rental non-real estate income (e.g., equipment leasing). It is important to consult with your CPA on how that information will flow into your tax return because the nomenclature here can be a bit misleading. For example, even though clause III 1 is labeled as "ordinary income/loss", it might still be passive for tax reporting purposes (e.g., if you were an LP in a syndication). And vice versa – just because rental income/ loss is reported in box III 2, it does not automatically mean it is passive (e.g., if you qualify as a real estate professional).

It is not uncommon for boxes 1 or 2 to show a loss in year 1 and 2 of operations, especially if the investment is eligible for cost segregation and bonus depreciation. This is one of the tax deferral benefits of investing in real estate syndications – even though the investment was profitable, the paper losses from depreciation reduce/eliminate the tax liability for that tax year thereby reducing one's effective tax rate.

Any distributions received throughout the year will be reflected in box III 19 and any interest income in box III 5.

Exhibit 16:

Part III **Partner's Share of Current Year Income, Deductions, Credits, and Other Items**

1	Ordinary business income (loss)	14	Self-employment earnings (loss)
2	Net rental real estate income (loss)		
3	Other net rental income (loss)	15	Credits
4a	Guaranteed payments for services		
4b	Guaranteed payments for capital	16	Schedule K-3 is attached if checked . . . . ☐
4c	Total guaranteed payments	17	Alternative minimum tax (AMT) items
5	Interest income		
6a	Ordinary dividends		
6b	Qualified dividends	18	Tax-exempt income and nondeductible expenses
6c	Dividend equivalents		
7	Royalties		
8	Net short-term capital gain (loss)		
9a	Net long-term capital gain (loss)	19	Distributions
9b	Collectibles (28%) gain (loss)		
9c	Unrecaptured section 1250 gain	20	Other information
		Z*	See Attached Stmt
10	Net section 1231 gain (loss)	AG	
11	Other income (loss)		
12	Section 179 deduction	21	Foreign taxes paid or accrued

Partnership tax returns and as such K1s are due by no later than 3/15. However, it is not uncommon for the partnership to file an extension, in which case the K1 may arrive after 3/15. Speaking from personal experience as an LP, there have been times when I received my K1s in July-August. Thus, I usually file a tax return extension. If extended the final personal tax return is due by 10/15 (if you invested via a business entity, the business tax returns are due by 9/15). However, your CPA must still do a prelim estimate of the tax liability at the time of the extension and if tax is due, it will be paid by 4/15 (or 3/15, if you invested via a business entity). Any refunds or adjustments will be settled at the time of the final return filing.

K-1s income/losses are subsequently reported on Schedule E of your personal tax return. This is where you will see the various K1 line items (non-passive and passive) listed.

I am not a tax advisor or a CPA, i.e., it is always best to consult with yours re your individual circumstances. However, I hope this high-level synopsis was helpful to clear up some of the confusions around K1s, their significance, how and where they fit in the overall tax documentation and the key sections to focus on when you review yours.

PART 7

MANAGING YOUR INVESTMENTS

CHAPTER 32

HOW TO MONITOR YOUR PASSIVE INVESTMENTS

Contrary to what the name suggests, passive investing is not truly hands off. While you are not necessarily involved in the day-to-day decision making, running the property, and executing on the business plan, you would still want to keep a pulse on your investment to ensure you are progressing towards your goals as planned and that the investment is performing as expected.

1. **Educate yourself and stay current on news and market updates.**

   It is important to have at least a basic understanding of the asset class, deal and market analysis as you evaluate investment opportunities. After all, you do not want to put your hard-earned money in a bad deal that enamored you with juicy returns. In addition, you want to understand the impact of macro, micro, and global economic events on real estate and the underlying investments, so you can proactively ask questions of your sponsor or raise those questions as part of your ongoing communication with them if they do not bring it up.

To empower and educate investors, I decided to write this book. In addition, I share educational content via my YouTube channel (https://www.youtube.com/@DreamBelieveAchieveRealEstate) and social media pages (LinkedIn, Facebook, Instagram).

2. **Review the monthly or quarterly updates prepared by the syndicator/fund manager** and do not be afraid to ask questions about the update itself or about market events and how the operator is handling or prepared to handle those (e.g., projection variance, macro events, interest rates, rising cost of insurance, etc.).

The ideal reporting package will include an executive summary outlining the key performance items or challenges and how they are being addressed, the complete financials (operating statement, balance sheet, and cash flow statement), p&l actual vs. the original underwrite projections, the general ledger, AR aging, AP aging, bank statements, loan statements, and rent roll. Ideally the report or comments would include an indication of the property value based on current market trends and DSC.

Just like you review your bank account or brokerage statement on a monthly basis, it is important to track how your LP investments are performing. This can also help you spot trends early and raise questions with the sponsor to discuss those ahead of time.

3. **Attend the periodic investor calls** (some are quarterly and some are annual) or at least watch the recording. Do not hesitate to follow up with question during or after the call. Such investor updates are designed to summarize key highlights of past performance and outline what lies ahead. In the 2022-2025 environment many of

those updates were setting the stage to better show and clarify why a capital call or pause of distributions may be necessary. Staying up to date would help you avoid surprises and presents an opportunity to discuss issues with the sponsor early on or conversely be prepared for an early exit (if the sponsor exceeds plan ahead of time), so you can be better positioned to have timely tax discussions with your tax advisor to maximize your gains.

4. **Track your investments**. Nowadays there are a variety of tools and systems. For example, Joe Fairless has a nice LP tracker (feel free to message me to request the link). Other platforms like Syndication Tracker and Vyzer help with that process too. Lastly, you can easily create one in Excel and tailor the columns to the key performance indicators important to you. It is great to check the investment tracker over time, especially as you start stacking up investments and seeing that additional income stream building out.

Passive investing is not truly passive as you should be a good steward of your money by staying engaged, monitoring the investment performance, and making sure you ask questions to stay up to date and stay informed so you can avoid surprises. This can also help you track how certain investments or operators are performing over time, which is a data point that can be useful for your next investing decision (and whether you want to continue working with that sponsor or invest in that market/asset class or if you should pivot). It is not an urgent activity but an important one to do (at least quarterly), so you position yourself and your passive investments for success.

CHAPTER 33

THE TYPES OF FINANCIALS STATEMENTS (AND WHY THEY MATTER)

When investing in a **fund or syndication**, understanding financial statements is key to evaluating the **credibility and accuracy** of reported financials. These statements provide insight into a company's financial health and transparency. I find that very often investors are not aware of the nuances across the various financial statement types and thought it would be important to spend some time to clarify those.

Below are the **four types of financial statements** you may encounter, ranked from the most basic to the most rigorous:

1. Company-Prepared Financials

These are **internally generated** by the owner or accounting team. In small businesses, they may even be self-prepared. They typically include:

- **Balance Sheet** – shows assets, liabilities, and equity
- **Income Statement** – outlines revenue and expenses
- **Statement of Cash Flows** – tracks cash movement

While useful, these financials **lack third-party validation**, so investors should review them carefully for accuracy and completeness. Supporting information such as the general ledger, bank statements, receivables and payables aging, the rent roll provided within the reporting package provides additional comfort.

Most syndications start with this type of financial statement.

2. CPA-Compiled Financials

A step up, **CPA-compiled** financials involve a Certified Public Accountant (CPA) taking internal records and organizing them into **formal financial statements**. However, the CPA does **not** review or verify the accuracy of the numbers—they simply compile the information.

This level is common for businesses **not yet ready for a full review or audit**, but looking to improve credibility with external investors.

Some syndications and most funds (at least until they reach a certain scale) provide this type of financial statement.

3. CPA-Reviewed Financials

At this stage, a CPA does not just compile the financials but **reviews them for accuracy and consistency**. They conduct:

- **Basic checks and validations** to ensure statements are reasonable
- **Limited assurance** that no material misstatements exist
- **Higher credibility** than compiled financials

Investors can have more confidence in CPA-reviewed financials, but they **still don't provide the highest level of assurance.**

Most larger funds or fund managers with multiple funds provide these types of financials, especially if requested by investors.

4. CPA-Audited Financials (The Gold Standard)

A **CPA-audited** financial statement is the most rigorous and trusted level. Here is why:

- **Thorough validation** – The CPA performs extensive checks and balances
- **Formal opinion issued** – Either "qualified" (issues found) or "unqualified" (clean)
- **Often legally required** – Many large funds and institutions must provide audited financials

For larger or more established investment funds, **CPA-audited statements are a must.** If you are investing in a new or smaller fund, you will likely encounter company-prepared or CPA-compiled statements, but as the fund grows, expect them to move toward CPA-reviewed or CPA-audited financials.

Why This Matters for Investors?

When evaluating an investment opportunity:

- **Start by asking for financials** – Know which type the fund provides
- **Understand the level of verification** – Compiled vs. reviewed vs. audited makes a difference

- **Prioritize transparency** – The more rigorous the financials, the lower the risk of hidden issues
- **Be aware that** the cost of such financials is paid for by the fund, i.e., distributions generated by the various syndications the fund is invested in are used to cover the cost of such financials (among other operating expenses).

Now that you understand the nuances across the various financials, you will be better equipped to make a decision on which type serves you best while balancing the cost of the fund/ syndication having to produce one.

CHAPTER 34

A PASSIVE INVESTOR'S GUIDE TO CAPITAL CALLS

A capital call (sometimes referenced as cash call) is a provision in the real estate investment structure that allows the sponsor to request (call for) additional capital. The meaning of capital call discussed herein is not the same as the capital call discussed in the Funds CHAPTER 25.

When the business plan progresses as planned and/or when the market cooperates, it is very rare that the sponsor team would need to make a capital call. However, as with any investment, there are risks involved. Thus, on occasion, the sponsors may have to call for additional capital. This is never a pleasant experience for anyone (GPs or LPs). Nevertheless, it might be the second-best option vs. letting the project get worse or having to rush and sell the property at a loss.

Usually the sponsorship team would/should contribute first. However, in certain situations their contribution might not be sufficient OR collectively they might not have sufficient capital due to low personal liquidity. This is when the call may extend to the LPs. How the GPs contribute the capital (equity vs. shareholder loan) may also require additional steps, such as obtaining lender approval.

Why would the sponsors issue a capital call?

There are many situations that might trigger a capital call. Below I will name a few.

The operator underestimated capex needed or had an unexpected event that resulted in more capex being required to complete the rehab (the likelihood of this happening with heavier lift projects is higher).

The operator did not raise enough capital upfront for operating reserves or depleted operating reserves for other purposes (e.g., large unexpected expenses like interest rate cap escrows, or funding cash shortfalls, etc.).

The market materially changed. The 2023-2025 environment is a case in point (marked by tariffs and high labor and materials costs). If the operator did not include sufficient cushion when underwriting the deal, such market events can adversely affect the property performance. For example - continuous and high increase in interest rates on a deal with floating debt; or high increase in commodity prices, resulting in material rise in materials and capex costs.

The property is underperforming due to a poor operator or poor property manager, resulting in higher vacancies or not achieving target rent increases.

What you need to know if a capital call occurs?

When a capital call occurs, you will receive written communication from the sponsor noting the dollar amount of the capital call or % of capital share and when the money is due.

The private placement memorandum (PPM) will outline the terms and conditions of a call and implication for lack of compliance (penalties or alternatives, see CHAPTER 24). As an LP you should ask questions and have the right to know how the capital call funds will be used and what triggered the call. You should be aware of the alternatives, including what happens should you not contribute (in which case dilution of your ownership share may be one consequence).

Lastly, ensure you understand the reasons behind the call as you never want to put more good money after bad. Thus, it is helpful to understand whether there is still equity in the deal, why the sponsor has chosen to infuse additional capital vs. perform a cash-in refinance or sell the property, timing of the turnaround, etc.

How to decide whether to participate in a capital call?

Ultimately the decision lies in your confidence with the sponsor's ability to execute on the updated business plan. It is important that the sponsor shares what caused the cash call and how the cash call will reposition the property for the better. **Treat each capital call as a net new investment** (since you are infusing net new cash into the deal). Therefore, follow a similar diligence process to understand the updated proforma (and how realistic the assumptions driving such proforma are), the market conditions and forecast, the sources and uses, and any changes in the capital stack post the cash call. It is also important to understand what the consequences are should the capital call not succeed. Lastly, confirm how much or what % the call the GP team is infusing as part of the cash call.

How do you mitigate a capital call as an LP?

Mitigating the risk of a capital call starts before you invest in a deal by vetting the sponsor, the deal, and the market upfront (discussed in Parts 3 and 4).

Familiarize yourself with the PPM, so you are aware of the capital call process and implications/alternatives in the beginning. Do not be afraid to ask your sponsor questions at the beginning of the process.

Continuous communication throughout the tenor of the deal is also key. You will be able to observe the progression of the business plan via the monthly or quarterly updates or your direct interactions with your sponsor. Thus, a capital call should not be a surprise if or when it occurs (unless the sponsor was withholding information, was not truthful, or committed fraud).

As with any investment, there are risks involved. The key is to identify the risk upfront and then determine how it can be mitigated and whether you want to proceed. This will help you avoid negative surprises if or when they occur. As I like to say, the only way to avoid risk is not to take one... though that might not be the best option either, if you want to grow and leave a legacy.

CHAPTER 35

ARE DISTRIBUTIONS A GOOD THING REALLY - A GUIDE FOR PAUSED DISTRIBUTIONS

One of the many reasons I like to invest in real estate is the benefit of cash flow, which usually comes in the form of monthly or quarterly distributions.

However, is receiving a distribution a good or a bad thing?

Our natural inclination is to think that it is a good thing. However, as usual, it is important to peel the onion a layer deep and look at the numbers.

The key question to answer here is: What is the source for that distribution – existing cash reserves OR cash flow from operations?

Before I opine, let's ensure we are all on the same page re what cash flow from operations is. That is the net operating income (measured as effective gross income less operating expenses) less debt service less asset management fees. The balance is cash flow available for distributions.

One may argue that capex should also be subtracted from that number. However, expenses for various capex projects in most cases are reserved for upfront and funded from the capex reserve account. If for any reason that is not the case, which raises other concerns, one should also subtract capex to arrive at the free cash flow number. [If the debt is amortizing, subtract any required principal payments. Lastly, subtract/add any working capital changes. This will give you the free cash flow number.]

Then compare the projected cash on cash return for the period to determine the amount of projected distributions. For example, a 10% cash on cash return in Year 3 on a $1,000,000 investor equity investment (for the entire deal) will result in total investors' distributions of $100,000.

Lastly, if the cash flow available for distributions is a positive number **and** exceeding the expected annual distribution (e.g., $100,000), as illustrated in the hypothetical number above, one can rest assured that the subject distributions are not coming from the rainy-day fund (partially or fully).

However, if they are partially or fully sourced from reserves on a consistent basis, this should not be a cause for celebration but rather a cause of concern. More specifically, it begs the question on what is causing the cash flow compression/negative cash flow and what plan the management team has to turn around the situation. If the problem remains unaddressed, reserves will be eventually depleted, leading management to make tough decisions, which include a high probability of a capital call.

On that note, another related question we are often asked is whether pausing distributions is a cause for concern. It will likely at a minimum raise a few questions the operators will need to address.

In some cases, the operator may pause distributions out of abundance of caution. An example of that is the period of

2022-2023, when there were certain operators performing well but faced with the unexpectedly rapid increase in interest rates and therefore forced to reserve/escrow extra for the purchase of future rate caps, as required by their lender OR simply pausing to accrue reserves for a potential refi (which in that environment given lower LTVs would have required a loan pay down). In some cases, the operator may also pause their asset management fee (and if vertically integrated may also lower the property management fee). This is not a happy moment but the more prudent strategy to preserve liquidity and weather the storm vs. doing a capital call a couple of months later. While distributions are paused, they are still accruing (assuming the deal was structured as such) and therefore payable once the project turns around.

In other cases, however, the asset is not only impacted by the rate environment but also by poor operations. In that case, pausing distributions slows the bleeding but does not resolve the underlying issue and even then, may eventually lead to a capital call or loss of the property. Aggressive underwriting and/or lack of operational expertise unfortunately led to foreclosures and capital calls for many assets in the space during that period.

Thus, while a pause of distributions may not necessarily be a happy moment, it might be the most prudent decision to make from a longer-term perspective and protection of the investor principal investment.

And as to receiving your monthly distributions.... well, make sure you check the operating statements and balance sheet to determine if you should be celebrating or picking up the phone and raising important questions to the sponsor.

CHAPTER 36

PREFERRED EQUITY PROS AND CONS

If you have been investing in syndications for a while, from time to time you may come across the term preferred equity or preferred equity partner. Perhaps you have not encountered this term before but may be curious about what it really means. Below I'll demystify just that, discuss some pros and cons, and share a couple of mitigating factors, so you can make an informed investment decision if or when you come across an investment structure that includes preferred equity.

But first, let's answer the question: **What is preferred equity?**

Preferred equity typically comes in the form of a large check contributing a material part of the capital in a deal. It is most commonly provided by an institution, a fund, or a family office. And as the "preferred" name implies, it not only ranks higher in the capital stack in terms of priority (see infographic below), but also carries preferred terms (in terms of preferred rate, voting powers, and potentially decision making).

Exhibit 17:

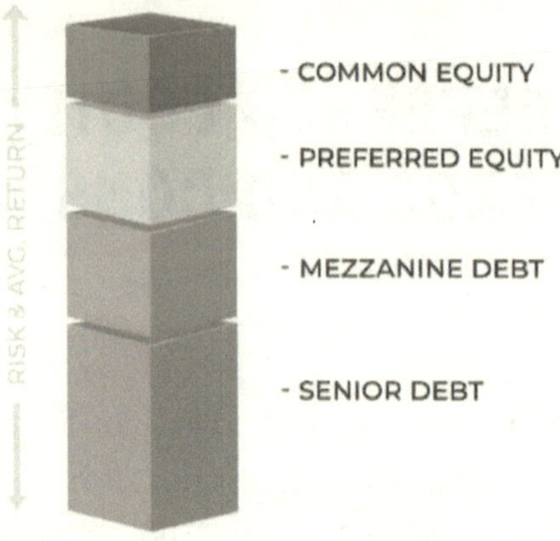

Why would one consider preferred equity after all? There are a couple of benefits:

First, it comes in the form of a large check from a single investor/ institution with deep pockets, which makes raising the capital a lot easier (and sometimes faster). In addition, the preferred equity investors are typically experienced and can bring additional expertise to the deal as well as additional liquidity, if needed (there are strings attached with that of course). Lastly, they provide institutional level oversight, which would enforce better reporting, communication, and operational discipline.

With all that, why would one decline or be concerned about having a preferred equity partner? A couple of drawbacks to consider include:

Given the size of their equity participation and voting/decision making rights, the preferred equity partners may have additional requirements and/or exercise undue influence on the deal to protect their investment and their rights. Such influence may not always be in the best interest of the passive investors (common equity LPs).

In addition, the preferred equity partner may walk away last minute with adverse consequences for the LPs. For example, they may determine last minute that they will only contribute 50% of the originally discussed check amount, leaving the syndicators to raise the rest at the eleventh hour. If the syndicators are unable to do so and still choose to close, it exposes the deal and the LPs to risk (e.g., not being able to raise the capex and operating reserves).

Another disadvantage to having a preferred equity partner is potential return dilution for the LP, especially when the preferred equity partner comes after close or if the preferred equity partner takes over the deal in a downside scenario.

Lastly, although not debt, given that in the capital stack it ranks ahead of equity and after debt and comes with fixed payments (the current pay is paid throughout the deal and the accrued pref is paid at the capital event/exit), it functions as quasi debt, i.e., it increases the leverage profile and therefore the risk profile of a deal.

Given the potential downside, how can one mitigate the risks involved with having a preferred equity partner?

It is important to understand the following:

- The terms of the agreement between the GPs and the preferred equity partner.
- Who the preferred equity partner is and their transaction (behavior) history.
- The economics of the deal.

It is also important for LPs to recognize that you are entering a deal with essentially three key decision makers – the lender first, the preferred equity partner second, and the operator third.

Ultimately do not move forward, if you are not comfortable with this and do not think the mitigates are sufficient. The beauty of investing is that you always have a choice whether to proceed or not, after you complete your own due diligence, recognize and analyze the risks involved, and understand (and get comfortable or not) with the downside.

CHAPTER 37

BENEFITS OF PORTFOLIO DIVERSIFICATION

I previously discussed key risks and mitigation strategies when investing in apartments. Risk management, however, further extends to managing risk within one's own portfolio as well.

How can one accomplish that? By being diversified. Diversification helps spread the risk and balance overall performance returns because in a real-world scenario not all investments will perform perfectly simultaneously over time.

In the beginning when you start investing, it is important to be focused to help prevent the feeling of being overwhelmed by numerous investment opportunities and being spread too thin to a point of inaction and analysis paralysis. However, as over time your portfolio starts to grow, it is important to manage concentration risk and consider diversification.

Below I share five key areas of diversification to consider.

1. **Sponsor.** In CHAPTER 21 I discussed how to find and connect with sponsors. Over time, you will likely build strong relationships with multiple ones. Asking for sponsor referrals from professionals and investors

within your network is another way to source such relationships over time.

2. **Market.** Real estate is regional and each market has its unique characteristics. Diversifying across various states or even cities within the same state is one way to approach spreading the risk. For example, states like TX and FL were more severely impacted by the rising cost of insurance in 2022-2023, which inevitably impacted the bottom line for many operators. Other states like IN or inland fared better, at least from a cost basis perspective. Considering the business/landlord friendly climate can also have a meaningful impact on performance.
3. **Asset Class.** In CHAPTER 38 I demystify other commercial real estate asset classes one can consider outside of multifamily, such as self-storage, industrial, commercial retail, etc.
4. **Asset Subclass.** Depending on one's risk appetite or investment criteria (cash flow vs. appreciation vs. tax mitigation) even within multifamily there are various opportunities to consider such as new construction, or build to rent, or opportunity zone investing, etc. in addition to the more traditional stable value add Class B apartment building.
5. **Funds.** Funds (discussed in CHAPTER 25) represent a great way to spread the risk. There are a variety of funds – ones that invest in the same asset class (multifamily for example) but in a variety of properties across markets or sub classes. Customizable funds allow one to further diversify across various asset classes within

the same fund, if the key sponsor makes such options available. Lastly, one can invest in a variety of funds – e.g., self-storage fund, short-term rental fund, etc. – and accumulate a fund portfolio over time.

Ultimately one's own risk appetite, investment objectives, and investment criteria will drive such decisions. However, the key is to not lay all your eggs in one basket and instead take calculated balanced risk and consider diversification as you progress along your investment journey.

PART 8

COMPARING ALTERNATIVES

CHAPTER 38

BEYOND MULTIFAMILY - OTHER CRE ASSET CLASSES EXPLAINED

One of the beauties of real estate is that there are not only various business strategies, but also a variety of asset classes to suit one's preference and risk appetite as well as to further diversify within real estate.

Should you look for ways to diversify beyond multifamily, there are many other asset classes to consider. Below I name a few, though the list is a lot longer than that.

Self-Storage: Rents storage space, also known as "storage units," to tenants, usually on a short-term basis. Self-storage tenants include businesses (commercial) and individuals (retail). Key items and terms to consider when evaluating self-storage deals include: population density, proximity to residential area, competition in the area, total square footage (vs. unit count), rent $/square foot, physical occupancy with reservations, seasonality, tenant mix (retail vs. commercial), online presence, staff, branding, property condition, opportunity for expansion, demand factors (for specific unit types), and smart tech. Self-storage is known as recession resistant as in theory when markets soften and people lose jobs, they downsize and need space to store personal property & possessions. In good times, as people accumulate personal property or move more, they need more space to store it. Commercial clients tend to like larger units relative to retail clients.

Mobile Home Parks: Rent pads (or the pad with the mobile home on it) within mobile park communities. Most were developed in the 1970s and are mom and pop owned. The lack of new inventory built creates scarcity. The age, coupled with many being run by mom-and-pop operators, create opportunity for value add and appreciation. Mobile home parks are graded on a 1-5 star scale, with 1 being the lowest/worst and 5 being the highest/best based on location, amenities, and condition. Key considerations to keep in mind include - number of units the mobile home park owns (park owned vs. tenant owned; preferably it will be park owned whereby the operator owns the pads only; banks would typically not lend on the unit itself as it is considered mobile personal property), location in need of affordable housing, utilities (avoid lagoons, septic tanks and wells). As mobile home parks are affordable, they are considered another recession resistant asset class.

Short- or Medium-Term Rentals: Renting a room by the night. Key metrics to watch for and understand include Occupancy, Average Daily Rate, Revenue Per Available Room, Location, and Seasonality. While hotels tend to be cyclical (as seen during the CV19 recession), short- or medium-term rentals performed well as people were looking for getaways away from dense urban areas. People also view short-term rentals as more convenient during travel (e.g., ability to be with the full family together or bring your pets). Medium term rentals provide more flexibility to certain tenant bases such as traveling nurses or digital nomads who may need the flexibility to rent on a shorter-term basis (vs. being tied to a 12-month or longer lease).

Commercial Retail and Industrial: Entail leasing shops, stores, restaurants, industrial warehouses. Key items to consider when evaluating such opportunities include credit quality of tenants and tenant mix, anchor tenants, lease rollover and built-in rent escalations, and common area maintenance (CAM) charges. Industrial properties (somewhat similar to multifamily) are graded on A (best) through C (worst) scale.

Special Purpose Properties: Include assisted living facilities, hotels/motels, hospitals or rehab facilities, data centers, cold storage, gas stations, churches, schools, parking lots, etc. Most entail also running and operating a business. Hence, the operator's background in operating such business (beyond real estate) is essential.

As you embark into other asset classes, just like with any investment, please ensure you are comfortable with the operator, market, business plan and understand how those assets are underwritten. These are the key ingredients.

CHAPTER 39

A COMPARISON OF SYNDICATIONS, CROWDFUNDING, REITS, AND REAL ESTATE FUNDS

For those interested in passive forms of investment there are several options. Below I outline the more common ones and the various aspects to consider as you determine which strategy is right for you.

Limited Partner (LP) in a syndication: As an LP, you invest directly in an LLC that owns a physical property asset (i.e., you are buying shares of a company that owns the property). Once you identify an operator and the asset class you want to invest in, you should allow some time to review the investment opportunity, do your diligence (as discussed in depth throughout the book), sign legal documents, and send your funds. As noted in CHAPTERS 26-27, syndications usually come with tax deferral benefits. However, they require meaningful upfront liquidity (minimum investment amount starts at $50,000 -$100,000) and are considered illiquid in nature (your investment is locked during the holding period of the asset and you cannot liquidate on a whim like you can with REITs or a Real Estate Mutual Funds).

Crowdfunding: With this type of passive investment, companies pool investor funds together with the purpose of investing in various real estate assets (single real estate assets). One of the key benefits is the lower upfront liquidity required – usual entry ticket can be as low as $1,000. Investors pay a management fee to the company organizing the crowdfunding deal. The fund managers make the decision as to timing, type and location of the property to purchase. They also (should) vet the operators. Similar to a syndication, this type of investment has a long-term investment horizon – the investor cannot liquidate on a whim. In addition, investors do not own a tangible asset or the ability to control the investments as they do with direct ownership. There are additional fees investors pay, which they would not otherwise incur if they invest directly in a syndication.

REITs (Real Estate Investment Trusts): REITs represent companies (the Trust) that purchase a number of real estate properties and form a portfolio, similar to a mutual fund (vs. holding standalone single assets). You invest in the company (the Trust) and the Trust owns and operates the underlying asset. REITs can be exchange traded, non-publicly traded, or private. The investors benefit from periodic dividend income (REITs are required to distribute 90% of their taxable income). Dividends are taxed as ordinary income, which can contribute to a larger, rather than smaller, tax bill. In addition, since you own a share of the portfolio and not the physical property, you do not directly benefit from depreciation, equity build up/appreciation, etc. (depreciation benefits are typically factored in prior to dividend payouts and as such, you cannot use depreciation expense to offset any of your other income). However, unlike syndications, the upfront liquidity required is smaller and investors can liquidate their REIT holding quickly (which also makes them prone to a similar volatility as the stock market).

Real Estate Funds (not to be confused with a syndication fund): Real estate funds are a type of mutual fund that invests in public real estate securities, sometimes including REITs (e.g., Fidelity Investments Real Estate Investment Portfolio Mutual Fund). Real estate funds are more of a long-term investment than REITs and provide their value through appreciation, rather than dividends. Unlike REITs, real estate funds tend to be more diversified and invest in many types of properties, not just commercial real estate. They are managed by professionals, which saves investors the trouble of having to do extensive research on where they should put their money. Similar to REITS, those investments can be liquidated quickly and do not come with added direct tax benefits (e.g., depreciation).

So which strategy is the best? After all, it depends on your personal investment objectives, investment horizon, liquidity, and desire for flexibility. The beauty of real estate is that there is no one size fits all approach. As such, you can apply a combination of strategies that best suit your individual circumstances and financial goals.

CHAPTER 40

KEY CONSIDERATIONS FOR INTERNATIONAL INVESTORS LOOKING TO INVEST PASSIVELY IN THE US

In prior chapters I discussed the various benefits of investing in real estate and syndications. It is not surprising then that such benefits when coupled with a more stable, regulated, and transparent US market as well as desire to diversify their investment holdings, investing passively in real estate becomes attractive to foreign investors. Depending on the amount of the investment and job opportunities created as a result thereof, for some it may even open a path to US residency.

However, there are a few important considerations related to tax, legal, compliance, and currency/capital constraints that foreign investors should keep in mind and plan ahead for when investing passively in the US.

1. **Consult with your tax advisor how best to invest – as an individual or a business entity and if via a business entity what type (LLC, LP, etc.).** Most foreign investors invest via LLCs; however, everyone's situation is unique

and, in some jurisdictions, (e.g., Canada, France, etc.) investing via an LLC may result in double taxation. Once you determine the type of legal entity, you will need to apply for an Employer Identification Number (EIN) as well as a Taxpayer Identification Number (unless you already have a Social Security Number). Your CPA and attorney can help you with the process.

2. **Consult with your tax advisor on whether you need to file a US tax return (federal and state) as a foreign LP and whether any tax withholding or treaty requirements will apply.** If investing via a foreign legal entity or as a non-US citizen/resident, be aware that it is not uncommon for the syndicator to withhold a tax. The withholding tax can be as low as 5% (if there is a treaty between the US and one's country) and as high as 30% (if no treaty; the IRS publishes the latest treaty information on their site). The withholding effectively forces the foreign entity or individual to file a US tax return to "claim" the withholding tax back if the income is ultimately not subject to US tax. Syndicators who do not withhold may be subject to penalty, i.e., as a passive foreign investor do not be surprised if the operator mentions the withholding tax requirements.
3. **Hire an attorney who can help with the US legal entity set up, including drafting the entity agreements.** Preferably such attorney will be real estate savvy and able to communicate in your native language, so he/she can also help you review the various documents you will be required to execute as an LP.
4. **Provide information as requested (to the CPA, attorney, bank, syndicator, etc.) to satisfy US compliance**

requirements (e.g., OFAC/PEP/BSA/AML/KYC). All physical and business entities are subject to those in the US.

5. **Open a US bank acct for the entity you are investing through (yourself or an LLC, for example). Your distributions and the capital gains from the investment will be deposited into that bank account.** Such account will likely also be used for transactional fees, e.g., paying CPAs and attorneys, etc. In most cases, you will need to open the account in person. This would be a good opportunity for you to visit the market or asset you are considering investing in and meet the local sponsor team(s). You may be able to invest via a foreign bank account as well. However, there is always a risk that the funds may be held in the correspondent banking system to go through additional compliance and no one has control on how long such funds may be delayed.
6. **Find out if you are subject to any capital restrictions** (e.g., certain countries have limitations on how much capital can be exported out of the country).
7. **Consider currency risk before or after the investment**, unless you already have USD savings accumulated ahead of time and plan to keep any gains in USD.
8. **Consider regulatory risk** – recall many Russian citizens' and businesses' bank accounts were frozen during the Ukraine/Russia conflict, which left many unable to access offshore liquidity easily.

The above may appear overwhelming, especially for new investors. However, fellow investors or the syndicator you are investing with may have referrals they can help connect you with to get started. In addition, setting up the bank accounts and legal entities as well as passing compliance and any other applicable regulatory approvals typically takes time. As such, you should plan for at least a 6–8-week lead time period until everything is set up (at least for your first syndication). Despite the additional steps, complexity, and time requirements, real estate investing can be an attractive investment opportunity for many across the globe and the long-term benefits can outweigh the upfront one-time set up costs, activities, and time.

PART 9

STAGES OF FINANCIAL FREEDOM

CHAPTER 41

THE PATH FROM FINANCIAL SECURITY TO FINANCIAL INDEPENDENCE (AND WHY YOU SHOULD NOT QUIT YOUR JOB SO FAST)

It all starts with a dream of who you want to be, what you want to accomplish, and why...and then believing in yourself and surrounding yourself with positive like-minded individuals... and last but not least, taking action!

You may often hear the terms financial freedom and financial independence used interchangeably. There is a subtle difference, however. Below I will review the different stages of reaching financial independence.

A good resource we have utilized for our own planning is Mandy McAllister's financial calculator, which is based on Tony Robbins' model - https://www.mandymcallister.com/post/financial-goals-calculator. It can be customized to your own financial situation and shows in a tangible way the number of properties one needs to acquire to reach that freedom number. You do not have to use a calculator of course. Knowing your monthly expenses well will help establish that initial baseline of what your (passive) income needs to cover (check out the quick calculation on how investing $50,000 can help you build a meaningful and tax efficient income stream over time later in this chapter).

Stage 1: Financial security - achieved when your income covers your basic needs of shelter, food, utilities, health insurance, and gas. It is imperative to start with the basics by setting a budget and making sure you live within your means and pay down bad debt. Bad debt is debt incurred to purchase items (outside of the ones noted above) that do not generate cash flow. Good debt is debt incurred to purchase cash flow producing assets, where the cash flow covers not only the debt service but other expenses associated with operating the property.

Stage 2: Financial vitality - achieved when the income covers all of the above expenses plus part of discretionary expenses for dining, clothes, entertainment, and other discretionary expenses.

Stage 3: Financial independence - achieved when income covers basic expenses plus all discretionary expenses for dining, clothes, entertainment, some luxury, and travel in full.

Stage 4: Financial freedom - achieved when income covers all of the above plus added luxuries and most importantly freedom of time to work when you want and wherever you want and how you want.

Real estate is just one tool (out of many) on how you can get on the path to generate additional income streams, build wealth, and ultimately achieve financial freedom. There are multiple paths to take and which one you choose is entirely up to you.

However, the key is to take action - take that first step, so you can get on the path of achieving financial freedom and reaching your own personal freedom (whatever freedom means to you). I am certainly glad that I overcame that fear and those limiting beliefs and the only regret I have is not starting sooner.

Understanding the stages of financial independence is important, but awareness alone does not create change. Many investors conceptually know what financial freedom looks like, yet remain stuck because they have not translated that vision into a clear and actionable plan.

The gap between financial security and financial independence is where most people spend the majority of their lives. It is not due to lack of intelligence or opportunity, but rather lack of structure, clarity, and consistent execution.

Once you have defined what each stage means to you and established your personal "freedom number," the next step is to move from theory to implementation. This is where intentional planning becomes critical - identifying income streams, allocating capital, setting timelines, and taking disciplined action over time.

In the following section, I will walk you through a practical five-step framework designed to help you create additional income streams, build optionality, and steadily progress toward financial independence and ultimately financial freedom.

1. **Get clear on your personal financial position** – amount of savings in the bank, amount of savings in retirement or brokerage accounts, monthly income (from all sources), and monthly expenses. Then review

your monthly expenses and determine the must have/ survival expenses that cover shelter, food, gas, and utilities, and some incidentals (see Financial Security above).

Ultimately the expense number one would need covered by passive income would vary from person to person depending on your lifestyle and individual goals. For some that freedom number would be the survival expenses. For others, it may include some additional expenses for travel and eating out or kids' education and healthcare. For third, the freedom number might equal one's current income.

2. **Next identify various passive income streams that cover this target freedom number.** In Chapter 42 below, I discuss how investing passively can generate a meaningful passive income stream. However, passively investing in syndications is just one income stream. Other income streams may include:
   - Being an affiliate (e.g., for Amazon or another product or service provider you recommend)
   - Providing consulting services on the side based on your area of expertise
   - Starting a franchise
   - Buying and managing a single-family rental, etc.

   I can speak in more detail to the passive investment in multifamily income stream as this is my area of expertise.
3. **Determine the amount of investable capital needed for any of these income streams.** In CHAPTERS 2,

18, and 30 I also discussed various sources of liquidity one can tap into, outside of standard savings. Another strategy I have seen couples deploy is to agree to live off the income of one spouse while using the other spouse's income to invest.

4. **Determine your freedom timeline.** Depending on your freedom number and amount of investable capital and time, for some this timeline may be 5-7 years and for others longer. However, once you have a timeline in mind, you can start tracking your progress against it to ensure you are continuously moving forward, one small step at a time. As real estate takes time, a 7–10-year time horizon at the very minimum is not atypical.
5. **Execute.** The most difficult part is usually taking action. Nevertheless, it is an important first step to get you started and to stay consistent over time. Set quarterly and annual personal financial meetings with yourself (or with your partner, as applicable). Life events may cause you to adjust the timelines. However, the important part is to track your progress over time, stay the course, adjust as needed, but keep moving forward. Real estate is **not** a get rich quick scheme. It does take time, hence the importance of getting started early.

Investing in real estate is just one vehicle one can use to achieve financial freedom and create job optionality. It was the path I chose and still remember the day when my passive income streams met and exceeded my survival expenses. Later that provided me with optionality to take on a path of serving others and being able to spend more time with loved ones. It did take time and certainly did not occur overnight or without careful planning but the upfront work paid off and it has turned out to be a rewarding journey.

CHAPTER 42

SAMPLE PASSIVE INVESTING INCOME CALCULATOR

Investing in real estate is by no means a get rich quick scheme. It takes time to build wealth over time through the power of cash flow and appreciation. I am sometimes asked how that can happen over time. Below I will show just that - how rolling over your passive investments can help you build wealth over time and set you well ahead on a path of pursuing your own freedom (whether that is retirement income or early retirement from your W2 job or whatever shape or form your own freedom takes).

Needless to say, there are events that may impact the performance of any investment, including real estate. As with any investment, it is important to recognize that there are risks, including the risk of total loss of capital. The only way to avoid risk of course is to not take one (but that is a topic for another book). However, to simplify the illustration and not overcomplicate it with multiple scenarios, permutations and combinations, I will make a few key assumptions. I will err on the more conservative side and assume returns will be on the lower end of the spectrum.

Assumptions:

- Cash on cash return of 5%
- Equity multiple of 1.5x
- Initial investment amount of $50K
- A new $50K investment is made every three years
- The principal investment is re-invested
- The investment performs as projected

Exhibit 18: The below example illustrates how one can accumulate approx. $30K in passive income over time.

Year		1	2	3	4	5	6	7	8	9	10
Investment 1	$50,000	$2,500	$2,500	$2,500	$2,500	$77,500	$3,875	$3,875	$3,875	$3,875	$120,125
Cash on Cash	5%										
Equity Multiple	1.5										
Investment 1	$50,000			$2,500	$2,500	$2,500	$2,500	$77,500	$3,875	$3,875	$3,875
Cash on Cash	5%										
Equity Multiple	1.5										
Investment 1	$50,000						$2,500	$2,500	$2,500	$2,500	$77,500
Cash on Cash	5%										
Equity Multiple	1.5										
Investment 1	$50,000									$2,500	$2,500
Cash on Cash	5%										
Equity Multiple	1.5										
Total annual income		$2,500	$2,500	$5,000	$5,000	$80,000	$8,875	$83,875	$10,250	$12,750	$204,000

Year	11	12	13	14	15	16	17	18	19	20
Investment 1	$6,006.25	$6,006.25	$6,006.25	$6,006.25	$186,193.75	$9,309.69	$9,309.69	$9,309.69	$9,309.69	$288,600.31
Cash on Cash										
Equity Multiple										
Investment 1	$3,875	$120,125	$6,006.25	$6,006.25	$6,006.25	$6,006.25	$186,193.75	$9,309.69	$9,309.69	$9,309.69
Cash on Cash										
Equity Multiple										
Investment 1	$3,875	$3,875	$3,875	$3,875	$120,125	$6,006	$6,006	$6,006	$6,006	$186,194
Cash on Cash										
Equity Multiple										
Investment 1	$2,500	$2,500	$77,500	$3,875	$3,875	$3,875	$3,875	$120,125	$6,006	$6,006
Cash on Cash										
Equity Multiple										
Total annual income	$ 16,256	$132,506	$ 93,388	$ 19,763	$ 316,200	$ 25,197	$ 205,385	$144,751	$ 30,632	$ 490,110

Assumes a 5-yr hold and a net new $50K investment every 3 years
Assumes the initial principal is reinvested
blue = indicates a number that can be changed

Needless to say, if the actual performance of the investment is on the higher end of the performance spectrum and/or if you start with a larger principal investment or if you invest every year (vs. every three years), the potential for annual income is even higher.

However, the example above intentionally uses lower numbers to align closer with current market reality and to illustrate the point that this process takes time and that not all investments perform as projected, i.e., this is NOT a get rich quick play.

Another way to back into the calculation is to think about the freedom number you established for yourself. For example, if your goal is $10K of monthly PASSIVE income, you will need to have $2.4MM deployed at all times in investments generating 5% cash on cash return or $1.2MM deployed in investments generating 10% cash on cash return. Most people do not start with $1MM and naturally the question arises on how to get there. Start small. That $100K if deployed in a deal that doubles the principal every 5-7 years, can turn into $1.6MM over a 20–30-year period (all else equal and if the investments perform as planned). And that timeline can be accelerated, if the amount and frequency of the invested principal is increased.

I hope the above quick analysis helped illustrate the power of investing in real estate over time. It certainly helped me visualize the potential outcome when I first started running the numbers. And it also helped demonstrate that achieving such desired outcome is well within reach. It requires patience and discipline. However, all one needs is to take action and get started. Making that first step is all it takes.

PART 10

CLOSING

CHAPTER 43

CONCLUSION

We covered a lot and I would encourage you to refer back to chapters you found interesting and use the content as a quick reference guide when you evaluate multifamily or commercial real estate investment opportunities.

Whether you read this book cover to cover or jumped to the chapters most relevant to you, you now have something most passive investors lack - a framework. You know how to assess a market, test the assumptions behind the numbers, evaluate the person behind the deal, and read the documents that govern your investment. You are no longer relying solely on someone else's spreadsheet or pitch deck to make decisions. You have a process you can trust and the confidence to use it.

That knowledge compounds over time, just like the investments themselves. Each deal you evaluate sharpens your judgment. Each question you ask strengthens your position. And each decision you make, including the decision to pass, brings you closer to building the kind of durable, passive income that creates real optionality for you and your family.

I want to personally thank you for taking the first step on educating yourself and becoming a well-rounded multifamily investor. I hope you decide to take action and take advantage of the benefits multifamily investing offers in order to further diversify your own portfolio and build a steady income stream that brings you closer to achieving financial freedom.

If you found this book beneficial, please share with a friend.

Remember to Dream. Believe. Achieve. Always.

Vessi Kapoulian

www.dbacapitalgroup.com

APPENDIX

INSIDER'S KIT

To access the complimentary resources that accompany this book, go to:

www.dbacapitalgroup.com/book-resources

For additional guidance on multifamily investing, go here: www.dbacapitalgroup.com

HOW TO EVALUATE A COMMERCIAL REAL ESTATE INVESTMENT OPPORTUNITY IN 5 MINUTES OR LESS

Once you have educated yourself on the basics of multifamily investing, how to get started, and begin to connect with various operators, you will start getting exposure to various investment opportunities. Some of you will feel the same excitement as a kid in a candy store. Others may get overwhelmed by how to quickly sift through these various investment opportunities coming through your inbox. In today's quick snippet, we will attempt to resolve some of that anxiety.

Let's assume that you have already vetted the operator, as you are on their email list.

Most investment opportunities presented via email will contain:

- a brief snippet describing the deal,
- a summary of projected returns,
- a link to the investor offering memo,
- a link to register for the upcoming webinar (or a recording of the webinar, in the event you missed the original one), and
- a direct link to invest.

The snippet is your first filter. It will typically have a picture of the property and will list:

- Asset Type: B+ Class, 120-unit multifamily
- Market: Orlando, FL
- Hold period: 5-7 years
- Minimum investment: $50,000
- Funding Deadline: By 12/31/2025

This information can quickly give you an idea of whether the opportunity meets your investment criteria of market, asset type and class, hold period during which your investment is locked into, amount of capital needed to participate, and how quickly the funds will be required. If you are at a low liquidity point or will not have the funds until three months later, then that is a quick pass. Alternatively, if the asset is in a market you are not keen on, that will help you quickly move on.

The next section will typically summarize the projected returns.

- Preferred return: 8%
- Average cash on cash return: 8%
- IRR: 15%
- Equity multiple: 2.0x

This information can quickly give you an idea of whether the opportunity meets your target investment returns.

Lastly, any mention of bonus depreciation can be another quick indicator whether this particular investment opportunity aligns with your tax and overall investment strategy.

As usual, you can always reach out to the sponsor who is sharing the investment opportunity with you to talk through it and address any questions you may have.

TOP 3 KPIS TO QUICKLY AND EFFECTIVELY VET A DEAL

I am often asked by fellow investors how to sift through the noise and the marketing materials of a deal presentation. I understand that the amount of information shared can be overwhelming. Therefore, below I offer three key performance indicators passive investors can focus on to determine if a deal is worth looking into further, particularly if you are a cash flow investor (you have to appreciate that for a detail-oriented individual, limiting myself to only three was an arduous task; 😊 the criteria below would not apply for equity yield investments such as new construction or a distressed deal, which might not generate cash flow for a couple of years).

1. **Positive Leverage.** Usually that is measured as the cap rate at purchase (unlevered return) is exceeding the all-in interest rate on the loan (cost of capital). I prefer to look at Yield on Cost (YOC) at stabilization instead as the YOC captures not only the purchase price, but also other costs associated with acquiring the property such as closing costs and capex. Thus, if the YOC exceeds the interest rate on the loan, this is usually a good indicator of positive cash flow and returns.

   For example, if a property is purchased at $22.75MM and generates actual trailing 12-month NOI of $1.475MM, the purchase price cap rate is 6.5% (=1.475/22.750). If closing costs and capex amount to $2.1MM and stabilized NOI is $1.8MM, then the YOC is 7.2% (=1.8/(2.1+22.75). Thus, a loan interest rate of 6.1% would yield positive leverage in both scenarios.

2. **Cash Flow on Day 1.** I measure that as rental income generated by the property today (assuming no increases in rent) vs. the sum of operating expenses (adjusted for increase in insurance and taxes) and debt service. If the NOI less debt service is positive, that is a strong position to start with. Bonus points if NOI meets the min 1.25x debt service coverage (which is the typical minimum set by lenders).
3. **Low Break-Even Occupancy Of 70% Or Less (and no more than 80%) once the property is stabilized.** The break-even occupancy is the sum of operating expenses and debt service divided by effective gross income. It effectively shows the amount of cushion, or in other words by how much can income reduce before it hits a level sufficient to solely cover opex and debt service. Any income below that level, would result in negative cash flow.

The common denominator across all three KPIs is cash flow, which is what covers the expenses and ultimately (along with the gain on sale) generates investor returns. Cash flow and cash reserves are the cushion that help an investment weather the storm during periods of market volatility. Hence, the importance to meet these KPIs on Day 1.

If a deal does not hit those KPIs but you still want to look into this further, it is worth a discussion with the sponsor to better understand the sources and uses for the transaction, how they are mitigating the thin or negative cash flow risk in the beginning, and why they still think this is a good investment.

Nevertheless, unless one is looking for higher risk, not meeting these hurdles on Day 1 would give one a pause, at least for me, as I like to invest for cash flow.

WHEN TO PASS ON A MULTIFAMILY OR COMMERCIAL REAL ESTATE INVESTMENT OPPORTUNITY

In this book I discussed how one can get started in real estate and how an initial $50K investment can be life changing. However, having that excess liquidity does not mean you should jump into every or any investment opportunity presented to you. Below, I will address key questions to think about before you decide whether to invest in a deal or not. You can also reference these questions as a checklist later on when you come across multifamily investment opportunities.

1. **What are the market dynamics and is the market conducive to the business plan?** For example, projecting a 10% rent increase for several years in a market with moderate population growth or projecting monthly rent of $1,700 in a market with median household income of $40K that realistically supports maximum rents of $1,100 is not a realistic assumption. At a minimum, it should cause you to pause and ask questions or ask the operator to substantiate their projection rationale.
2. What is the track record of the operator running similar projects? What is the track record of the sponsorship

team? Who is the extended team, especially the property manager (and if applicable the day-to-day asset manager), and what is their background?

3. **What is the property and its condition and do the numbers align with that?** Class C properties generally require more maintenance due to their age – is that reflected in the repairs and maintenance number? Is the property a heavy value add or a light value add? Do the capex projections align with the nature of the value add required to generate positive returns? Does the hold period align with the nature of the value-add strategy?
4. **How conservative is the underwriting and does it align with the market fundamentals?** (See CHAPTER 17 for details on this topic. You can also refer to www.MasteringMultifamilyUnderwriting.com/Book for a more in-depth discussion on deal analysis.)
5. How does the debt structure align with the business plan?
6. **Does the return align with the level of risk?** For example, a lower IRR may be appropriate for a stabilized or a light lift property. A heavy value add or turnaround strategy should yield higher returns as it carries more risk. How much of the return is generated from cash flow vs. appreciation?
7. **Does the opportunity align with your own investment objectives (cash flow, appreciation, tax shelter, etc.), target returns, investment horizon, and liquidity position?** Generally speaking, unless this is within your own risk tolerance, you should not be investing your last

dollar into a deal. These investments have a medium to long-term horizon and cannot be liquidated overnight, in the event of a personal emergency.

Needless to say, as with any investment, there are risks involved. There are exogenous events, outside of one's control or foresight (especially when one is projecting 3-7 years out), that could adversely impact the investment – high and continuous increase in interest rates, high inflation, a recession or depression, a natural disaster, regulations, etc. In extreme circumstances or in events where the risks were not mitigated upfront or there was not sufficient cushion/margin of error built into the numbers, the business strategy may pivot from generating the projected returns to preserving capital or minimizing losses.

TOP 5 ATTRIBUTES OFTEN OVERLOOKED BY PASSIVE INVESTORS

In CHAPTER 21 I discussed key questions to ask when vetting a sponsor and additional resources passive investors can use to pre-screen a sponsor. Below I will cover five factors passive investors often overlook when screening a sponsor and making a decision on who to invest with.

1. **Scaling too fast.** Are the sponsors purchasing multiple properties, scaling too fast without proper infrastructure and collecting fees? Doing multiple deals may be ok if they have the people and process infrastructure and can demonstrate that they are thoroughly vetting each deal vs. pursing any deal that crosses their desk. It is not uncommon for certain sponsors to partner with multiple operators. In that scenario, you want to ensure they are properly vetting each operator.
2. **Not having skin in the game or a strong track record.** Skin in the game incentivizes the sponsor not only to perform detailed upfront diligence, but also to stay engaged throughout the tenor of the investments and focus on operations and execution of the business plan post close. Being a Key Principal is one way to show skin

in the game, as these are the individuals who often sign on the loan and would ultimately be liable, if the loan converts from non-recourse to recourse. Providing a personal guarantee is another way sponsors can show skin in the game because if such guarantee is called on, the sponsor may have to liquidate personal assets. Lastly, bringing in personal liquidity to a deal also shows commitment to the investment, as such personal investment is at risk, if the deal does not progress as planned.

3. **Lack of diversification.** While it may feel comfortable to work with a sole sponsor, it is advisable to diversify across sponsors, geographies and asset classes to mitigate the risk of a market or a single sponsor or asset class getting in trouble. Another way to mitigate that is via a (customizable) fund; however, not every sponsor offers that option.
4. **Infrequently or not at all monitoring investment performance.** While investing passively does not entail running the day-to-day operations, you want to track your investment's results over time to see how it performs relative to the returns projected at inception. This also helps the passive investor spot declining trends early and have a conversation with the sponsor, in the event that trend is not discussed in the periodic investor communications. Lastly, if you do not receive monthly or quarterly updates from the sponsor, ask for them from your designated sponsor contact.
5. **Not asking for references.** It is not uncommon to share current and past investor references, so long as sponsors

have permission to do so (certain investors may choose not to be publicly cited for privacy concerns). In most cases, obtaining a reference, should not be an issue however. In addition, passive investors may not be compensated for providing a reference on their sponsor. This helps ensure you are getting an honest view when you reach out to them for a reference on your contemplated sponsor.

The key to a successful investment starts upfront during the vetting process. As a passive investor, you are not expected to be an expert on the market, deal analysis, or property operations. This is why it is even more important to complete diligence on the sponsor and think through your investment strategy.

THE FOUR REAL ESTATE CYCLES EXPLAINED

I frequently mention that real estate goes through cycles. And while real estate is also regional, i.e., one market may be expanding while another one may be in decline, the core four stages of a cycle usually carry similar characteristics. In today's quick snippet, I will demystify these four real estate cycles.

Exhibit 19:

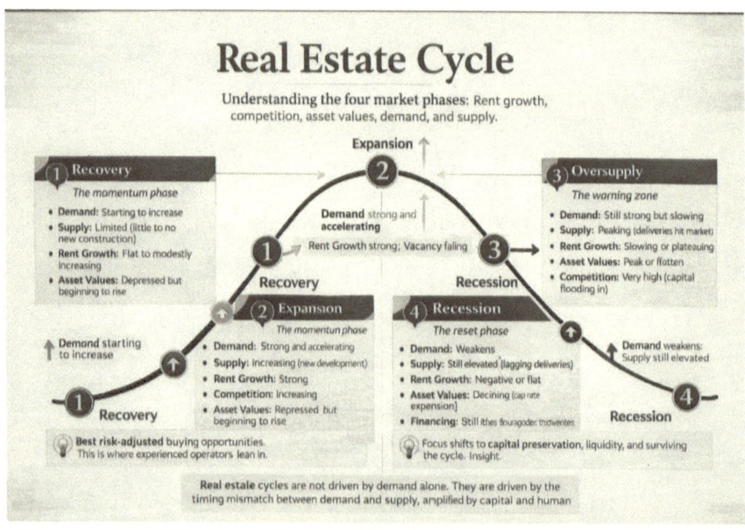

1. **Recovery**. At this stage of the cycle, it may not always feel as recovery. Some investors may still be on the sidelines

and new construction starts may be nominal. Properties may be operating below the long-term average market occupancy rates. Rents are still subdued but starting to grow as demand starts to recover. This is a good time to buy. Given the early stage of this cycle, taking on value-add Class B or C+ properties creates a tremendous opportunity to capitalize on upcoming appreciation in the next stage of the cycle.

2. **Expansion.** At this stage of the cycle investors are feeling more optimistic and are jumping back in. New construction starts and completions are ramping up. Rents and occupancy are climbing above the long-term historical average. It is a great time to buy a Class B value add property to force further appreciation.
3. **Oversupply.** Due to overbuilding or due to economic factors, rents and occupancy levels start to decline. There may still be frenzy in the market and some investors believe the recession is farther away or that "it will be different this time". It is a good time to sell non-core or non-performing assets before it is too late.
4. **Recession.** At this stage of the market, investors are sitting on the sidelines and feel doom and gloom. Rents are continuing to decline and occupancy rates are below the long-term average occupancy and declining. Valuations are near the bottom too. It may be a good time to purchase distressed assets at more reasonable valuation, especially if the goal is to hold such assets long term and wait out the next cycle as long as there is cash flow.

It is important to understand which part of the cycle you are in, in order to position accordingly. As each market or asset class may be at a different stage of the cycle, it is important to have a diversified portfolio to manage through such cycle fluctuations. Lastly, as transition periods between cycles may be difficult to spot when they occur, it is important to underwrite conservatively at all times, as a way to mitigate such fluctuations.

GLOSSARY OF KEY TERMS

Acquisition Fee (2-5% of purchase price) – typically paid to the General Partners (GPs) at the close. However, in some scenarios, some GPs may choose to invest the proceeds in the deal or may delay collection of the fee until a certain Limited Partner (LP) return is achieved. GPs would often review many deals before they find the one where the numbers make sense. This process will often entail additional expenses, such as travel, earnest money deposits gone hard on a deal they ultimately chose to walk away from, diligence reports/reviews on a deal that did not move forward, etc. The acquisition fee partially compensates GPs for that effort and the aforementioned out-of-pocket costs.

Additional collateral support typically includes personal guarantees from the sponsors or key principals. Some lenders (agencies) may also have certain requirements, e.g., the guarantor(s) must possess (combined) liquidity (cash and marketable securities) equal to a minimum of 10% of the loan amount and (combined) net worth equal to the loan amount. When the loan requires a personal guarantee, it is also known as a recourse loan.

Amortization/Amort

Debt amortization is the process of paying off a loan through scheduled, pre-determined installments that include principal and interest.

For example: 30-yr straight line amortization on a $300,000 loan would equate to annual principal payment of $10,000. Based on that schedule, the loan would be fully paid off in 30 years.

Average Annual Return (AAR)
Return **on** investment *averaged over the hold period of the asset,* measured as total cash flow distribution to members throughout the tenor of the deal plus the capital gain at the time of sale divided by the principal amount divided by the hold period.

Example:

Initial investment amount: $100,000.

Total cash distributions and capital gain received at the time of sale: $100,000.

Hold period: 5 years.

AAR is calculated as follows -

($100,000 profit /$100,000 principal amount) / 5 years = 20% AAR

Asset Management Fee (1-2% of effective gross or of net income) – typically paid out of the monthly cash flow. It compensates the GP for the time and effort involved in actively managing the asset to ensure execution against the original business plan progresses as scheduled.

Basis points (bps)

Equals 1/100 of 1%.

Examples: 10 bps = 0.10%; 25 bps = 0.25%; 50 bps = 0.50%, 100 bps = 1%, etc.

Break-Even Occupancy

Calculated as total operating expenses plus debt service divided by effective gross income.

Measures at what point of occupancy revenue generated by the property covers the property expenses (including debt service) just enough to break even.

May see that measured as both unit count and %.

A break-even of 80-unit count on a 100-unit property for example, simply means that occupancy can decrease from 100 to 80 units before it breaks even.

Similarly, a break-even of 80% simply means economic occupancy can drop to 80% before the property breaks even.

Capital Expenditures (Capex)

The amount spent on improving a property.

An example would be: replacing roofs, updating electrical, painting the building, updating interior units.

It is best that the capex reserves are raised upfront and NOT relying on cash flow from operations to fund capex.

Cap Rate

The rate of return on a real estate investment property based on the income such property generates/is expected to generate AND if purchased all cash.

Factors affecting the cap rate:

- underlying economic or market conditions

- interest rates
- demand for and supply of the underlying asset
- asset class
- location
- building age and condition, etc.

Usually, the higher the risk profile of the asset, the higher the expected cap rate will be. Think higher risk – higher return.

Where to find market cap rate – broker reports, CoStar, appraisals, being active in the market, apartmentloanstore.com

Cap rate compression means cap rates are decreasing, i.e., values are rising.

Cap rate reversion (decompression) means cap rates are increasing, i.e., values are declining.

Entry Cap Rate or Purchase Price Cap Rate = Actual (in-place) NOI at time of purchase/ Purchase Price.

Exit Cap Rate = Actual (in-place) NOI at time of sale/ Sale Price.

Market Cap Rate = cap rate at which properties are trading at in the market today.

Cash Flow After Debt Service/CAPEX/AM Fees

Usually shows that net profit (NOI) after Debt Service, Capex, and Other fees (e.g., asset management fees).

Cash flow available for distributions is NOI less Debt Service less Asset Management Fee. If capex is not reserved for upfront, then capex also needs to be subtracted from the number above to determine the amount of distributable cash.

Cash On Cash Return (CoC)

Cash income earned relative to the original cash investment. The original cash investment typically includes the down payment on a loan (if the property is financed), closing costs, capex reserves, and operating reserves.

For example, a property generating $10,000 in annual cash flow after debt service and initial cash investment of $100,000, has a 10% cash on cash return.

Closing costs and fees, including exit fees

These are the typical fees required for diligence and processing the transaction and may include but not limited to: appraisal/environmental/seismic/property condition reports, underwriting fees, lender legal fees, title and title insurance fees, escrow, etc.

Collateral

This is the asset that you pledge to secure the loan. In the event of foreclosure, the lender can step in and sell the asset in order to fully or partially pay off the loan balance and eliminate or reduce their losses, respectively. Sometimes a lender may require the owner to cross collateralize certain properties (usually if the subject asset is in a more distressed position). When cross collateralizing properties be careful because you are typically not allowed to pledge properties that are already encumbered by another lender. In addition, if the subject property fails, you are at risk of losing the cross-collateralized properties too.

Construction Management Fee (5-10% of rehab budget) – for properties that may require more work to turn around in a short period of time, it serves to compensate the GP during that transition period for managing contractors, leasing efforts, and the property manager.

Contract Rent: The Rent is the rent being charged and collected on existing leases at a property. In contrast to Market Rent, contract rent is not based on market conditions but rather is based on the lease contract signed between the landlord and tenant.

Core (Class A) Properties that are: Built in the last 10-15 years. The highest quality. Modern construction. Lowest amount of deferred maintenance. Premium and several amenities (gym, dog park, office, community room, pool, spa, etc.). In excellent locations, good school districts, high income-low crime areas. Tenant base is white collar or high income. Command the highest rent. More sensitive to recessions; tenant base may transition to a Class B property during a recession. A higher purchase price, lower cash on cash return, lower but more stable cash flows, and the greatest potential for appreciation, lowest level of risk. Cap rates tend to be the lowest.

Core Plus (Class B) Properties that are: Built in the last 15-30 years. Construction is generally of good quality. May be brought up to a Class B+ or Class A level after substantial renovation and modernization. Opportunity for forced appreciation via value-add updates. Some deferred maintenance. Fewer amenities. Located in stable neighborhoods and moderate income and low to moderate crime areas. The tenant base is a mix of middle-income professionals and higher earning blue collar workers. Rents are moderate. Less expensive than Class A properties.

Moderate cash on cash return, moderate cap rate, moderate to high appreciation and moderate risk.

Covenant structure

To monitor loan performance and establish early triggers in the event of property deterioration, most lenders would have loan covenants (financial and reporting). The most typical financial covenant is a minimum DSCR. The most typical reporting requirements are the annual operating statement, rent roll as well as any other reports required from the loan guarantor, if the loan is recourse-based. Some lenders (typically the agencies) will also have opening requirements like min property occupancy of 90% for the 90 days preceding close, cap on tenant concentrations, etc.

Debt Service

The amount spent to service the debt. Usually the sum of the principal and interest. For interest only loans, it is the sum of interest.

Debt Service Coverage Ratio (DSCR)

The Annual NOI divided by Debt Service. Lenders usually require a minimum of 1.25x. Effectively it measures ability of the cash flow generated by the property (NOI) to service the debt (debt service).

Debt Yield

Debt yield is calculated as NOI divided by the loan amount. In essence, it represents the inverse of the property's cash flow leverage position. Lenders may apply this as they determine the loan size.

Disposition Fee (1-2% of the sale price) – typically paid at close/ sale. It compensates the GP for the work put into preparing the property for sale and coordinating the sale to completion.

Economic Vacancy

The amount of occupied but non-paying units. Examples include – concessions, bad debt, employee units, etc.

Effective Gross Income

Equivalent to Net Revenue. Represents the gross income minus physical & economic vacancy plus other income.

Effective Rent

Actual rent charged, after concessions and discounts. Could also be referenced as in-place rent but should not be confused with contract rent (defined above).

Equity Multiple (EM)

Measured as total dollars received divided by total dollars invested. Total dollars received includes the cash flow earned throughout the hold period of the asset coupled with the sale proceeds.

For example, if you invested $100,000 and you received a total of $200,000 throughout the hold period of the asset including gain on sale and return of your principal, that means you achieved equity multiple of 2.00x or in other words you doubled your initial investment.

Garden Style Apartment

Garden-style apartments are low-rise, spread-out communities with outdoor entrances and landscaped settings, designed to feel more residential and less urban.

Gross Potential Rent

The maximum potential rent one can charge based on current market. May also be labeled as "market rent" on the T12.

Guarantor Fee (1-2% of the loan amount) – typically paid at close and designed to compensate the guarantor for putting up their personal balance sheet behind the deal. The guarantor may or may not choose to be involved in the day-to-day operations.

Therefore, they would want to be extra comfortable with the operators' ability to execute before signing the dotted line with their name. If the deal was to go bad, their name would be on the line.

Internal Rate of Return (IRR)

IRR is the discount rate that makes the net present value (NPV) of all cash flows equal to zero. In other words, it's the expected compound annual rate of return that will be earned on a project or investment. It captures the time value of money.

Less meaningful metric for forever buy and hold projects (CoC may be a better KPI for such projects).

Interest Only (IO)

The period during which the loan does NOT amortize and incurs only interest payments due.

Interest rate

The interest rate on the loan can be fixed (for part or the entire loan tenor) or floating (usually based on an Index like SOFR, BSBY, Prime, etc. plus a loan spread). If you choose a floating rate but are looking for ways to hedge the risk of rising interest rates you can use financial derivatives like swaps (a swap fixes the index rate) or options (collars (set a rate floor and a rate cap) or caps (set a cap on how high the index rate can increase)) to mitigate such risk. Banks may have capabilities to offer both swaps and options. Other loan providers may only be able to offer options.

Investment Offering Memo

The investment offering is prepared by the lead sponsor team and details the investment opportunity. It is a marketing document (often referred to as pitch deck). It outlines the team, the market, the property, the financial aspects of the deal (including fees and projected returns), key risks, sensitivity analysis, and how to join the investment. The official investment is typically documented via the Private Placement Memorandum (PPM).

KPI = Key Performance Indicator

Loan Assumption

When one operator assumes the loan of another upon takeover of the property.

Key Considerations When Evaluating a Loan Assumption

- Sponsor strength
- Loan balance
- Loan tenor
- Loan amortization
- Interest-only period remaining, if any
- Interest rate, fixed or floating
- Min DSC

- Loan assumption fees
- Negotiate a discount when you are doing the seller a favor – e.g., assuming a higher rate loan
- Beware of the exit cap rate assumptions (especially when assuming a low interest rate loan in a higher cap rate environment)
- Usually, a 1% loan assumption fee is assessed by the lender

Loan Broker Fee (1-2% of the loan amount) – typically paid at close and designed to compensate the mortgage broker for the work put in to solicit the best financing terms and position the deal for success to the ultimate lender.

Loan sizing

While LTV is most commonly cited in prelim term sheets as a loan sizing metric, lenders would typically size the loan based on cash flow. Therefore, it is not uncommon for lenders to size the loan on the *lesser of* LTV, DSC, and Debt Yield.

Loan To Value (LTV)

Calculated as the amount of the loan divided by the property value. Often referred to as leverage.

Example: Loan amount of $1.5MM and property value of $2.0MM, would result in LTV of 75%.

Loan providers

The usual loan providers in the commercial real estate space are banks, agencies (Fannie Mae and Freddie Mac), commercial mortgage-backed securities providers (CMBS), and insurance companies. They each have varying tolerance of risk and property type requirements; therefore, each will usually have varying loan structures.

Loan types

The two most typical loan structures are bridge (short-term, 1-3 years) and permanent (aka perm 3+ years).

LOI (Letter of Intent)

A document that outlines the preliminary terms and basic framework of a potential deal or transaction before a formal, legally binding contract is created. It is usually non-binding and serves as a roadmap for future negotiations, helping to streamline discussions and determine if the parties are aligned before committing to a final, formal agreement.

Loss/Gain to Lease

The difference between the maximum potential market rent and actual rent.

Loss to Lease indicates there is additional potential to increase rent.

Gain to Lease indicates we are leasing at above market rates.

Market Rent

Usually listed on the rent roll. Indicates the market (typical/ comp) rent for that particular unit type and size. It does not represent the maximum potential rent necessarily.

Mill

A "mill" is 1/1,000 of a dollar, or $1 for each $1,000 of assessed value. A mill is used to calculate a property's millage rate.

Millage Rate

The millage rate is used to calculate the property tax on real property. This is calculated in increments of $1,000, with each mill representing 0.1% of the property's taxed assessed value, which is often lower than market value. For example, if a property's tax assessed value is $20,000,000 and has a millage rate of 20, then its property tax would equate to $400,000 ($20 for every $1,000 of value). In many jurisdictions, the millage rate is converted to a percentage (mill rate ÷ 1000) and quoted as a property tax rate for ease of calculation.

Mortgage Constant

A rate calculated by dividing the periodic loan payment by the initial loan amount. The Mortgage (or Loan) Constant is often used as a tool to efficiently calculate loan payments and is represented as a percentage. For instance, a mortgage loan with an annual payment of $16,000 and an initial loan balance of $250,000 has a Mortgage Constant of 6.40%. In an interest only loan, this metric would be the same as the interest rate where with an amortizing loan this would be different because there are principal payments included as well.

Net Absorption

In the case of for lease property, net absorption is the rate at which rentable area is leased up over a period of time in a given market. The net absorption figure considers construction of new space, demolition of existing space and any additional vacancies during that period. It is often used to forecast demand and supply trends and is thus a key indicator for both property owners and developers, significantly influencing their pricing and timing decisions.

Net Operating Income (NOI)

Equivalent to Operating Income of a business. Effective Gross Income (Rent) minus Operating Expenses.

In-place NOI = actual NOI (this is what lenders underwrite to).

Stabilized NOI = NOI reached when the property is stabilized (e.g., at market vacancy and rents and optimized expenses).

Occupancy

The number of occupied units.

Occupancy %: Occupied units as % of Gross Rent. The inverse of vacancy %.

Offering Memo (OM)

The memo, usually prepared by a commercial broker, that presents the deal, the investment opportunity, the market, and brief financial overview of the property.

Operating Expenses (Opex)

The necessary and ordinary expenses incurred to operate the property.

Examples include: Admin, Advertising, Contract Services, Insurance, Labor, Legal, Property Management, Repair & Maintenance, Replacement Reserves (usually imposed by the lender), Tax, Turns, Utilities, etc.

Operating Expense (Opex) Ratio (OER)

Operating Expenses divided by Effective Gross Income.

Usually ranges from 35-60%. Could be as low as 35% for brand new properties OR 60%+ for older properties with deferred maintenance. Most common is 50%.

HOWEVER, the ratio varies by market and property.

Opportunistic (Class D): Properties that are described as war zones. The roughest properties one can encounter. Constructed in the last 30-100 years. Often in poor condition and plagued with much deferred maintenance. No amenities. Located in the roughest part of town marked with violence, drugs, and prostitution. The tenant base is low income and may have a criminal record. The least expensive and the riskiest and as a result will offer the highest cash on cash return. Cash flow may be volatile. Even if upgraded, based on the property location, they will rarely appreciate in value and essentially have no exit plan. They represent the highest level of risk.

Other Income

Additional income generated by the property.

Examples: Pet Rent, Utility Bill Back, Laundry, Late charges, Parking, Valet Trash, etc.

Passive Investor

Often also referred to as the Limited Partner or LP. The investor is providing the capital and relying on the operator/lead sponsor/general partner (GP) to manage the investment with the goal and expectation for probable future profits.

Physical Vacancy

The amount of non-occupied/vacant units.

Positive/Negative Leverage

Positive Leverage: When cap rate (or YOC) exceeds the loan interest rate. In other words, when the unlevered return exceeds the cost of capital.

Example: Cap rate of 6.5%. All in interest rate of 6%.

Negative Leverage: When the cap rate (or YOC) is below the loan interest rate. In other words, when the unlevered return does NOT exceed the cost of capital.

Example: Cap rate of 5%. All in interest rate of 6%.

Positive leverage is a good prelim indicator of positive cash flow.

If leverage is negative, then it might be best to buy the property all cash (vs. finance).

Preferred Return

A profit distribution preference whereby profits, either from operations, sale, or refinance, are distributed to one class of equity before another until a certain rate of return on the initial investment is reached.

Typically calculated on an annual basis and on the principal amount invested.

Typically paid first before any profit splits (promote) kick in.

Preferred returns are not guaranteed and depend on the cash flow generated by the property. As such, it is important to understand how they are treated in the event there is a shortfall.

The most typical structure is cumulative, i.e., the preferred balance due, if unpaid, carries over into the next year. LPs may not receive the return as planned but will not lose on it (unless the overall investment suffers a loss). And if it keeps accumulating till sale, such cumulative preferred return accrued to the LPs will be typically paid fist (after the loan and associated transaction fees as well as the invested principal amount), followed by the LP's share of the gains, and lastly the GP's share of the gain.

Cumulative and compounding is another method, whereby the preferred return not only accumulates over time, but the rate is calculated on the accrued balance (vs. the original principal balance). This method is less common and certainly more beneficial for the LPs.

Preferred return may be **calculated on returned or unreturned capital contribution principal amount.** This is why it is important to understand whether distributions constitute return on capital (most common) or return of capital (less common).

Prepayment penalties

It is not uncommon for loans to have penalties if the loan is paid off prior to the maturity date. Penalties can be structured differently (defeasance, yield maintenance, step down, etc.). Thus, it is important to understand the prepayment penalty structure upfront.

Promote

This is typically an outsized share of the profits, payable once the investors have received back their entire initial capital contributions and achieved certain profit thresholds (i.e., preferred return).

Promote is also referred to as the promoted interest or carried interest. Refers to how the profit splits/share on a syndication are structured. For example, a 30% promote would typically mean that 70% of profits go to the limited partners (passive investors) and 30% of profits go to the general partners (sponsors, syndication team).

Refinance Fee (1-2% of the loan amount) – typically paid at the close of the refi. It compensates the GP for managing the loan refi process, which would include soliciting proposals, evaluating and selecting the optimal refi terms, working with the lender and property manager to provide the needed information to complete the refi, and coordinating post-close activities related to returning of capital to the LPs.

Re-margin provisions

This requirement is more typical for banks vs. agencies. It effectively may require the owner to pay down the loan to bring LTV or DY within a certain hurdle in a scenario where market values decline.

Ratio Utility Billing System (RUBS)

A method of calculating a resident's utility bill based on specific factors such as occupancy rate or apartment square footage and then billing the tenant for their share of utility use.

SOFR (Secured Overnight Finance Rate)

SOFR replaced LIBOR (London Interbank Offered Rate) after the LIBOR scandals and is now the market rate often used by banks and other financial institutions for lending purposes on US-Dollar denominated contracts. It fluctuates daily and can have various tenors – daily, 1-month, 3-month, 6-month. SOFR's cousins include: SONIA (for GBP denominated loans), €STR (Euro), TONA (Japanese Yen), SARRON (Swiss Franc), CORRA (Canadian Dollar), SORA (Singapore Dollar), and AONIA (Australian Dollar).

Sponsor

This is the lead syndicator, the key operator leading and controlling the deal. They are often referred to as the General Partner or GP. This is the person (or people) who are responsible for the sourcing, management, and the disposition of the deal. Passive investors (LPs) rely on the GP's efforts to generate possible profits from the investment.

Stabilization period

The period of time required to reposition the asset from the time of purchase to a steady eddy run rate. Typically, 24-36 months for larger (150+ unit) assets or 12-18 months for smaller assets (10-50 units).

Stabilized NOI

The NOI run rate reached after the property is stabilized, i.e., after the repositioning activities are completed.

Tax

When and how they are assessed can vary from county to county. They can be assessed at the point of sale (POS), annually, every 3-5 years, etc.

How they are assessed can vary from county to county - % of the purchase price, mileage rate based on assessed property value (usually measured as % of the original purchase price).

Tenor

The loan tenor is the loan maturity date. While it is not uncommon to have a 30-year tenor for residential loans (1-4 units), for most commercial real estate the tenor is shorter (3-10 years) leaving a balloon payment due at maturity. This is not something to panic about. In most cases, at maturity the owner would either refinance the property (thereby extending the tenor) or sell the property (thereby paying off the loan with the sale proceeds).

Value Add (Class C) Properties that are: Built within the last 30-50 years. Have average to low functionality, typically outdated and in need of remodel. Have much more deferred maintenance and limited (if any) amenities. Opportunity for forced appreciation. Located in lower income-moderate crime areas. Opportunity may be found in Class C properties located in Class B areas.

Rental rates are low to moderate. The tenant base typically is comprised of blue collar/working class households. Turnover and vacancy tend to be higher. Less expensive than Class B properties.

Offer higher cash on cash return, higher cash flow, low to moderate appreciation, and pose higher risk. Cap rates tend to be higher.

Yield On Cost

The unlevered rate of return on an asset based on the all-in cost.

Calculated as Stabilized NOI divided by the All-In Cost of a Property (Purchase Price + Capex + Closing Costs).

CAN YOU HELP?

Thank You for Reading My Book!

I really appreciate all of your feedback, and I love hearing what you have to say.

Your input to make the next version of this book and future books better would help many.

Please leave me an honest review on Amazon letting me know what you thought of the book.

With gratitude,

Vessi Kapoulian

www.ingramcontent.com/pod-product-compliance
Lightning Source LLC
LaVergne TN
LVHW091254150826
845673LV00006B/1409